Fabulous
Baseball Facts,
Feats, and
Figures

THE POLO GROUNDS
NEW YORK

NEW YORK

SEASON OF 1887.

HOME GAMES OF THE NEW YORK BALL CLUB FOR THE LEAGUE CHAMPIONSHIP.

April 28, 29,	with	Philadelphia,
May 5, 6, 7,	"	Boston,
" 9, 10, 11,	"	Washington,
" 14,	"	Philadelphia,
" 16, 17, 18,	"	Indianapolis,
" 20, 21, 23, 24,	"	Pittsburg,
" 26, 27, 28,	"	Detroit,
Decoration Day " 30 A.M. & P.M. 31,	"	Chicago.

June 9, 10, 11,	with	Washington,
" 13, 14, 15,	"	Philadelphia,
July 7, 8, 9,	"	Detroit,
" 11, 12, 13,	"	Pittsburg,
" 15, 16, 18,	"	Chicago.
" 19, 20, 21,	"	Indianapolis,
" 23, 25, 26.	"	Boston,

Aug. 22, 23,	with	Pittsburg,
" 25, 26, 27,	"	Chicago,
" 29, 30, 31,	"	Indianapolis,
Sept. 1, 2, 3,	"	Detroit,
" 5, 6, 7,	"	Washington,
" 26, 27, 28,	"	Boston,
Oct. 5, 6, 8,	"	Philadelphia.

FABULOUS BASEBALL FACTS, FEATS, AND FIGURES

By Joseph L. Reichler
Foreword by Pete Rose

COLLIER BOOKS
Division of Macmillan Publishing Co., Inc.
New York

COLLIER MACMILLAN PUBLISHERS
London

Some of these tables previously appeared, in slightly different form,
in *The Great All-Time Baseball Record Book*,
by Joseph L. Reichler (Macmillan, 1981).

Macmillan Publishing Co., Inc.
866 Third Avenue, New York, N.Y. 10022
Collier Macmillan Canada, Ltd.

Printed in the United States of America

10 9 8 7 6 5 4 3 2 1

First Collier Books Edition 1981
Fabulous Baseball Facts, Feats, and Figures
is also published in a hardcover edition by
Macmillan Publishing Co., Inc.

Library of Congress Cataloging in Publication Data
Reichler, Joseph L., date
Fabulous baseball facts, feats, and figures.
Includes index.
Summary: Lists more than 100 baseball records,
including most hits per game, most career shutout
games, unassisted triple plays, team records,
and Cy Young award winners.
1. Baseball—United States—Records—Juvenile
literature. [1. Baseball—Records] I. Title.
GV877.R38   796.357'64'0973   81-6019
ISBN0-02-044720-5 (pbk.)   AACR2

Table of Contents

PITCHING RECORDS   **65**

FIELDING RECORDS 107

List of
Picture Essays

List of Abbreviations

Team Abbreviations

ATL	Atlanta	MIN	Minnesota
BAL	Baltimore	MON	Montreal
BOS	Boston	NY	New York
BKN	Brooklyn	OAK	Oakland
BUF	Buffalo	PHI	Philadelphia
CAL	California	PIT	Pittsburgh
CHI	Chicago	PRO	Providence
CIN	Cincinnati	SD	San Diego
CLE	Cleveland	SEA	Seattle
DET	Detroit	SF	San Francisco
HAR	Hartford	STL	St. Louis
HOU	Houston	SYR	Syracuse
IND	Indianapolis	TEX	Texas
KC	Kansas City	TOR	Toronto
LA	Los Angeles	TRO	Troy
LOU	Louisville	WAS	Washington
MIL	Milwaukee	WOR	Worcester

Statistical Abbreviations

A	Assists	LF	Left Fielder
AB	At Bats	LH/RH	Left-Handed or Right-Handed
BB	Bases on Balls		
1B	Singles or First Baseman	MVP	Most Valuable Player
2B	Doubles or Second Baseman	OF	Outfielder
3B	Triples or Third Baseman	Opp.	Opponent
C	Catcher	P	Pitcher
CF	Center Fielder	Pct.	Percentage
CG	Complete Games	PO	Putouts
Cons.	Consecutive	Pos.	Position
Diff.	Difference	R	Runs Scored
DP	Double Plays	RBI	Runs Batted In
E	Errors	RF	Right Fielder
ERA	Earned Run Average	SB	Stolen Bases
FA	Fielding Average	2nd	Finished Second
G	Games	ShO	Shutouts
H	Hits	SO	Strikeouts
H/A	Home or Away	SS	Shortstop
HBP	Hit By Pitch	SV	Saves
HR	Home Run	TB	Total Bases
Inn.	Inning	TC	Total Chances
Inns.	Total Innings in Game	W	Wins
IP	Innings Pitched	Yrs.	Years
L	Losses		

In the tables a blank indicates a repeated name, team, or date. If the number of innings is not listed, it is 9.

History of the Teams

AMERICAN LEAGUE

| Baltimore Orioles (1954–) | St. Louis Browns (1902–53) | Milwaukee Brewers (1901) |

Boston Red Sox (known as Somersets 1901–4, (1901–)   Puritans 1905–6)

| California Angels (1966–) | Los Angeles Angels (1961–65) |

Chicago White Sox (1901–)

Cleveland Indians (known as Bronchos 1901, Blues 1902–4, (1901–)   Naps 1905–11, Molly McGuires 1912–14)

Detroit Tigers (1901–)

Kansas City Royals (1969–)

| Milwaukee Brewers (1970–) | Seattle Pilots (1969) |

| Minnesota Twins (1961–) | Washington Senators (1901–60) |

| New York Yankees (known as Highlanders 1903–12) (1903–) | Baltimore Orioles (1901–2) |

| Oakland Athletics (1968–) | Kansas City Athletics (1955–67) | Philadelphia Athletics (1901–54) |

Seattle Mariners (1977–)

| Texas Rangers (1972–) | Washington Senators (1961–71) |

Toronto Blue Jays (1977–)

NATIONAL LEAGUE

| Atlanta Braves (1966–) | Milwaukee Braves (1953–65) | Boston Braves (1876-1952) (known as Red Caps 1876–82, Beaneaters 1883–1906, Doves 1907–8, Pilgrims 1909–11, Bees 1936–40) |

Chicago Cubs (1876–) (known as White Stockings 1876–93, Colts 1894–97, Orphans 1898)

Cincinnati Reds (1890–) (known as Red Legs 1944–45)

Houston Astros (1962–) (known as Colt .45s 1962–64)

| Los Angeles Dodgers (1958–) | Brooklyn Dodgers (1890–1957) (known as Bridegrooms 1890–98, Superbas 1899–1910) |

Montreal Expos (1969–)

New York Mets (1962–)

| Philadelphia Phillies (1883–) (known as Blue Jays 1943–44) | Worcester Nationals (1880-82) |

| Pittsburgh Pirates (1887–) (known as Alleghenys 1887–89, Innocents 1890) | Louisville Colonels (1892–99, merged with the Pirates in 1900) |

St. Louis Cardinals (1892–) (known as Browns 1892–97)

San Diego Padres (1969–)

| San Francisco Giants (1958–) | New York Giants (1883–1957) (known as Gothams 1883–85) | Troy Trojans (1879–82) |

Foreword

Even though I'm a ballplayer myself, I'm still a real baseball fan, and as a fan I loved reading this book.

When I flip through the pages, I see all the great records since they started playing baseball, the ones everyone knows about. But this book also has a lot of new records I'd never seen listed before. My friend Joe Reichler is great at digging up the kinds of things you don't see every day—all the unassisted triple plays, all the pitchers who struck out four batters in an inning, all the players who stole second, third, and home in one game. (Like me.)

But what makes this book so great is that it's got all those great players. The ones my father used to tell me about, like Walter Johnson and Babe Ruth, the ones I saw when I was growing up, like Ted Williams and Jackie Robinson, and the ones I've been lucky enough to play against, like Willie Mays and Hank Aaron. They're all here, with all the records that compare today's stars to the great old-timers.

Joe Reichler is the only person I know who could have written this book. He used to be a sportswriter, and now he's a special assistant to the Commissioner of Baseball, but what really counts is that Joe is one of the greatest baseball fans ever. He's been collecting all these facts and figures for years, and now he's put them all together for you to read and enjoy.

I know you'll have as much fun reading this book as I did!

Pete Rose

Batting
Records

One Saturday in the early autumn of 1881, Roger Connor made baseball history. Troy was playing Worcester, and Worcester was leading 7–4. Up came Connor, with the bases loaded. He walloped a home run to give Troy an 8–7 victory. Connor's blast was the first grand-slam home run in major league history.

Since then, thousands of grand slams have been hit. Ernie Banks and Jim Gentile have each hit five in one season, and seven players have hit two grand slams in one game. Tony Lazzeri of the 1936 New York Yankees was the first. Two players, Bill Duggleby of the 1898 Phillies and Bobby Bonds of the 1968 San Francisco Giants, connected for grand slams in their first major league games. Duggleby's came in his very first at bat—what a way to start a career!

Most Grand Slams, Career

Player	Total
Lou Gehrig	23
Willie McCovey	18
Jimmie Foxx	17
Ted Williams	17
Hank Aaron	16
Babe Ruth	16
Gil Hodges	14
Joe DiMaggio	13
Ralph Kiner	13
Ernie Banks	12
Rogers Hornsby	12
Joe Rudi	12
Rudy York	12
Hank Greenberg	11
Harmon Killebrew	11
Lee May	11
Willie Stargell	11
Joe Adcock	10
Johnny Bench	10
Roy Sievers	10
Al Simmons	10
Vern Stephens	10
Vic Wertz	10

Every batter dreams of hitting a home run with the bases full. When the batter is a pinch hitter coming off the bench at an important moment, it's even more of a dream come true.

The first pinch-hit grand slam was made by a pitcher, Mike O'Neill of the St. Louis Cardinals, in a game against the Boston Braves on June 3, 1902. The first American League pinch-hit grand slam came on September 24, 1916. Marty Kavanaugh, a utility infielder for Cleveland, hit a hard liner off Hub Leonard of the Boston Red Sox. The ball rolled through a hole in the fence, and everyone scored.

Only two players have hit pinch grand-slams in both leagues—Jimmie Foxx and Roy Sievers.

Most Pinch-Hit Grand Slams, Career

Player	Team	Date	Total	Opp.	Opp. Pitcher
Ron Northey	STL N	Sep 3, 1947		CHI	Doyle Lade
	STL N	May 30, 1948		PIT	Elmer Singleton
	CHI N	Sep 18, 1950	3	BKN	Dan Bankhead
Willie McCovey	SF N	Jun 12, 1960		MIL	Carl Willey
	SF N	Sep 10, 1965		CHI	Ted Abernathy
	SD N	May 29, 1975	3	NY	Bob Apodaca
Rich Reese	MIN A	Aug 3, 1969		BAL	Dave McNally
	MIN A	Jun 7, 1970		WAS	Dick Bosman
	MIN A	Jul 9, 1972	3	NY	Lindy McDaniel
Jimmie Foxx	PHI A	Sep 21, 1931		DET	Tommy Bridges
	PHI N	May 13, 1945	2	STL	Ken Burkhart
Bill Skowron	NY A	Aug 17, 1954		PHI	Al Sima
	NY A	Jul 14, 1957	2	CHI	Jim Wilson
Gene Freese	PHI N	Apr 18, 1959		CIN	Mike Cuellar
	PHI N	1959	2	CIN	Jim Brosnan
Yogi Berra	NY A	Jun 7, 1953		STL	Satchel Paige
	NY A	Jun 23, 1962	2	DET	Phil Regan
Vic Wertz	BOS A	Aug 14, 1959		NY	Ryne Duren
	BOS A	Aug 25, 1960	2	CLE	Don Newcombe
Roy Sievers	CHI A	Jun 21, 1961		CLE	Johnny Antonelli
	PHI N	May 26, 1963	2	CIN	Bill Henry
Ed Bailey	SF N	Jun 26, 1962		CIN	Joey Jay
	SF N	Apr 10, 1963	2	HOU	Don McMahon
Davy Johnson	PHI N	Apr 30, 1978		SD	Bob Shirley
	PHI N	Jun 3, 1978	2	LA	Terry Forster
Mike Ivie	SF N	May 28, 1978		LA	Don Sutton
	SF N	Jun 30, 1978	2	ATL	Dave Campbell

PINCH HITTING

The first pinch hitter in baseball history was Mickey Welch, a pitcher for the New York Giants, who came to bat in an emergency on August 10, 1889. He struck out. Two years later, the rules of baseball were changed to allow substitute batters at any time, not just when a player has been injured.

Jack Doyle recorded the first pinch hit for Cleveland on June 7, 1892. Pinch hitting has since become an important part of the game. Manny Mota has the most pinch hits, 150. Jose Morales holds the record for pinch hits in a season, with 25 for Montreal in 1976. Tommy Davis has the highest lifetime batting average as a pinch hitter, .320. The top single-season average for hitters with 15 or more pinch hits is .486, by Ed Kranepool of the 1974 Mets.

Manny Mota of the Los Angeles Dodgers, the all-time leader in career pinch hits. In 1980, at the age of 42, Mota came through with 3 hits in 7 pinch appearances during a tight pennant race.

Tom Daly of Brooklyn, batting for Hub Collins in the ninth inning against Boston, connected for the first pinch-hit home run in baseball history on May 14, 1892.

Pinch homers were few and far between in the early years of baseball. But as the ball was made livelier and easier to hit for distance and pinch hitters became more common, pinch-hit home runs became less of a rarity. It's a rare season now when there aren't at least 50 pinch homers in the two leagues.

Jerry Lynch (*left*) was one of the first pinch-hitting specialists, setting a record by hitting 18 career pinch-hit home runs. Thanks to his pinch-hitting ability, **Smokey Burgess** (*right*) was able to extend his career. In his last three years with the White Sox, he appeared in 236 games but played in the field in just 7.

BATTING RECORDS

Most Pinch-Hit Home Runs, Career

Player	Total	Player	Total
Jerry Lynch	18	Champ Summers	8
Cliff Johnson	16	Del Unser	8
Gates Brown	16	Gavvy Cravath	7
Smoky Burgess	16	Tito Francona	7
Willie McCovey	16	Oscar Gamble	7
George Crowe	14	Clarence Gaston	7
Joe Adcock	12	Jim Hart	7
Bob Cerv	12	Harmon Killebrew	7
Fred Whitfield	11	Lefty O'Doul	7
Cy Williams	11	Rip Repulski	7
Don Mincher	10	Bob Skinner	7
Wally Post	10	Duke Snider	7
Gus Zernial	10	Earl Torgeson	7
Norm Cash	9	Jerry Turner	7
Gene Freese	9	Johnny Blanchard	7
Bobby Hofman	9	Mickey Mantle	7
Dale Long	9	Ted Williams	7
Mike Lum	9	Walker Cooper	6
Ken McMullen	9	Jim Hickman	6
Jose Morales	9	Jay Johnstone	6
Ron Northey	9	Rick Joseph	6
Carl Sawatski	9	Reggie Jackson	6
Bill Skowron	9	Andy Kosco	6
Vic Wertz	9	Danny Litwhiler	6
Bob Allison	8	Ernie Lombardi	6
Brant Alyea	8	Sam Mele	6
Ed Bailey	8	Merv Rettenmund	6
Johnny Frederick	8	Hank Sauer	6
Frank Howard	8	Art Shamsky	6
Lee Lacy	8	Dick Stuart	6
Charlie Maxwell	8	Ron Swoboda	6
Johnny Mize	8	Bob Thurman	6
Bill Nicholson	8	Ed Kranepool	6
Roy Sievers	8		

Ever since Babe Ruth hit 60 home runs in the 1927 season, the number 60 has stood for baseball's most glamorous record, one which seemed almost unbreakable. The closest anyone had come to the Babe's record was in 1938, when Hank Greenberg socked 58 home runs in his first 150 games, but he was held without a homer in his last five games to fall two short. (One game had ended in a tie.)

But records are made to be broken, and in 1961, Roger Maris of the New York Yankees broke through the magic 60 barrier with his sixty-first home run on the last day of the season. Ruth-worshipers point out that Maris made his mark in a 162-game season, while Ruth hit his in only 154 games. But it's easy to get too caught up in the records. Maris may have broken Ruth's record, but Ruth is still the greatest slugger the game has ever known.

BATTING RECORDS

Most Home Runs, Season, AL

Player	Team		HR	Player	Team		HR
Roger Maris	NY	1961	61	Gorman Thomas	MIL	1979	45
Babe Ruth	NY	1927	60	Jimmie Foxx	PHI	1934	44
	NY	1921	59	Hank Greenberg	DET	1946	44
Jimmie Foxx	PHI	1932	58	Harmon Killebrew	MIN	1967	44
Hank Greenberg	DET	1938	58	Carl Yastrzemski	BOS	1967	44
Babe Ruth	NY	1920	54	Frank Howard	WAS	1968	44
	NY	1928	54		WAS	1970	44
Mickey Mantle	NY	1961	54	Ted Williams	BOS	1949	43
	NY	1956	52	Al Rosen	CLE	1953	43
Jimmie Foxx	BOS	1938	50	Hal Trosky	CLE	1936	42
Babe Ruth	NY	1930	49	Gus Zernial	PHI	1953	42
Lou Gehrig	NY	1934	49	Roy Sievers	WAS	1957	42
	NY	1936	49	Mickey Mantle	NY	1958	42
Harmon Killebrew	MIN	1964	49	Rocky Colavito	CLE	1959	42
Frank Robinson	BAL	1966	49	Harmon Killebrew	WAS	1959	42
Harmon Killebrew	MIN	1969	49	Dick Stuart	BOS	1963	42
Jimmie Foxx	PHI	1933	48	Babe Ruth	NY	1923	41
Harmon Killebrew	MIN	1962	48	Lou Gehrig	NY	1930	41
Frank Howard	WAS	1969	48	Babe Ruth	NY	1932	41
Babe Ruth	NY	1926	47	Jimmie Foxx	BOS	1936	41
Lou Gehrig	NY	1927	47	Hank Greenberg	DET	1940	41
Reggie Jackson	OAK	1969	47	Rocky Colavito	CLE	1958	41
Babe Ruth	NY	1924	46	Norm Cash	DET	1961	41
	NY	1929	46	Harmon Killebrew	MIN	1970	41
	NY	1931	46	Reggie Jackson	NY	1980	41
Lou Gehrig	NY	1931	46	Ben Oglivie	MIL	1980	41
Joe DiMaggio	NY	1937	46	Hank Greenberg	DET	1937	40
Jim Gentile	BAL	1961	46	Mickey Mantle	NY	1960	40
Harmon Killebrew	MIN	1961	46	Rico Petrocelli	BOS	1969	40
Jim Rice	BOS	1978	46	Carl Yastrzemski	BOS	1969	40
Rocky Colavito	DET	1961	45		BOS	1970	40
Harmon Killebrew	MIN	1963	45				

The pressures on **Roger Maris** *(opposite page),* standing here in center field of Yankee Stadium next to the monument to Babe Ruth, took all the fun out of the game. Reporters hounded him, and the Babe's many fans didn't want to see him break the record. "All it brought me was headaches," he later said.

The short, stocky slugger **Hack Wilson** banged out 56 homers in 1930 for the National League season record.

BATTING RECORDS

Most Home Runs, Season, NL

Player	Team		HR	Player	Team		HR
Hack Wilson	CHI	1930	56	Ernie Banks	CHI	1957	43
Ralph Kiner	PIT	1949	54	Davy Johnson	ATL	1973	43
Willie Mays	SF	1965	52	Rogers Hornsby	STL	1922	42
George Foster	CIN	1977	52	Mel Ott	NY	1929	42
Ralph Kiner	PIT	1947	51	Ralph Kiner	PIT	1951	42
Johnny Mize	NY	1947	51	Duke Snider	BKN	1953	42
Willie Mays	NY	1955	51	Gil Hodges	BKN	1954	42
Ted Kluszewski	CIN	1954	49	Duke Snider	BKN	1955	42
Willie Mays	SF	1962	49	Billy Williams	CHI	1970	42
Willie Stargell	PIT	1971	48	Cy Williams	PHI	1923	41
Dave Kingman	CHI	1979	48	Roy Campanella	BKN	1953	41
Mike Schmidt	PHI	1980	48	Hank Sauer	CHI	1954	41
Ralph Kiner	PIT	1950	47	Willie Mays	NY	1954	41
Eddie Mathews	MIL	1953	47	Eddie Mathews	MIL	1955	41
Ted Kluszewski	CIN	1955	47	Ernie Banks	CHI	1960	41
Ernie Banks	CHI	1958	47	Darrell Evans	ATL	1973	41
Willie Mays	SF	1964	47	Jeff Burroughs	ATL	1977	41
Hank Aaron	ATL	1971	47	Rogers Hornsby	CHI	1929	40
Eddie Mathews	MIL	1959	46	Chuck Klein	PHI	1930	40
Orlando Cepeda	SF	1961	46	Ralph Kiner	PIT	1948	40
Ernie Banks	CHI	1959	45	Johnny Mize	NY	1948	40
Hank Aaron	MIL	1962	45	Gil Hodges	BKN	1951	40
Willie McCovey	SF	1969	45	Ted Kluszewski	CIN	1953	40
Johnny Bench	CIN	1970	45	Duke Snider	BKN	1954	40
Mike Schmidt	PHI	1979	45	Eddie Mathews	MIL	1954	40
Ernie Banks	CHI	1955	44	Wally Post	CIN	1955	40
Hank Aaron	MIL	1957	44	Duke Snider	BKN	1957	40
	MIL	1963	44	Hank Aaron	MIL	1960	40
Willie McCovey	SF	1963	44	Willie Mays	SF	1961	40
Hank Aaron	ATL	1966	44	Richie Allen	PHI	1966	40
	ATL	1969	44	Tony Perez	CIN	1970	40
Willie Stargell	PIT	1973	44	Johnny Bench	CIN	1972	40
Chuck Klein	PHI	1929	43	Hank Aaron	ATL	1973	40
Johnny Mize	STL	1940	43	George Foster	CIN	1978	40
Duke Snider	BKN	1956	43				

Another of the Babe's "unbreakable" records was his lifetime total of 714 home runs. For 40 years, no one came within 100 home runs of this awesome figure. But then along came Henry Aaron.

Aaron ended the 1973 season with 713 homers. On Opening Day, 1974, Aaron tied Ruth's record with his first swing of the bat. The record finally fell three days later, when Aaron knocked Al Downing's pitch into the bullpen for home run number 715 and baseball immortality. He ended his career two years later with 755 home runs.

Who was the better home-run hitter, Aaron or Ruth? Ruth hit 714 home runs in 8,399 at bats—one home run every 11.6 at bats. Aaron ended his career with 755 homers in 12,364 at bats—one every 16.4 at bats. So the argument goes on.

Most Home Runs, Career

Player	HR
Hank Aaron	755
Babe Ruth	714
Willie Mays	660
Frank Robinson	586
Harmon Killebrew	573
Mickey Mantle	536
Jimmie Foxx	534
Ted Williams	521
Willie McCovey	520
Eddie Mathews	512
Ernie Banks	512
Mel Ott	511
Lou Gehrig	493
Stan Musial	475
Willie Stargell	472
Billy Williams	426
Carl Yastrzemski	419
Reggie Jackson	411
Duke Snider	407
Al Kaline	399

Hank Aaron watches the flight of his historic 715th home run. With this blow, Aaron established himself as baseball's leading home run hitter.

Mike Schmidt of the Phillies set a record for home runs in one season by a third baseman when he hit 48 in 1980.

Most Home Runs by Position, Season, AL

Player	Team		Pos.	HR
Hank Greenberg	DET	1938	1B	58
Joe Gordon	CLE	1948	2B	32
Al Rosen	CLE	1953	3B	43
Rico Petrocelli	BOS	1969	SS	40
Roger Maris	NY	1961	OF	61
Yogi Berra	NY	1952	C	30
	NY	1956		30
Gus Triandos	BAL	1958		30
Wes Ferrell	CLE	1931	P	9

Most Home Runs by Position, Season, NL

Player	Team		Pos.	HR
Johnny Mize	NY	1947	1B	51
Davy Johnson	ATL	1973	2B	43
Mike Schmidt	PHI	1980	3B	48
Ernie Banks	CHI	1958	SS	47
Hack Wilson	CHI	1930	OF	56
Roy Campanella	BKN	1953	C	41
Don Newcombe	BKN	1955	P	7
Don Drysdale	LA	1958		7
	LA	1965		7

BATTING RECORDS

Most Home Runs by Position, Career, AL

Player	Pos.	HR
Lou Gehrig	1B	493
Jimmie Foxx		473
Norm Cash		375
Joe Gordon	2B	253
Bobby Doerr		223
Charlie Gehringer		183
Graig Nettles	3B	273
Brooks Robinson		267
Sal Bando		232
Vern Stephens	SS	227
Joe Cronin		151
Rico Petrocelli		129
Babe Ruth	OF	686
Ted Williams		521
Mickey Mantle		496
Yogi Berra	C	313
Bill Dickey		202
Bill Freehan		180
Wes Ferrell	P	36
Red Ruffing		35
Earl Wilson		35

Most Home Runs by Position, Career, NL

Player	Pos.	HR
Willie McCovey	1B	440
Gil Hodges		355
Orlando Cepeda		334
Rogers Hornsby	2B	289
Joe Morgan		224
Bill Mazeroski		138
Eddie Mathews	3B	481
Ron Santo		334
Ken Boyer		263
Ernie Banks	SS	293
Pee Wee Reese		124
Leo Cardenas		117
Hank Aaron	OF	661
Willie Mays		643
Mel Ott		475
Johnny Bench	C	323
Roy Campanella		242
Gabby Hartnett		233
Warren Spahn	P	35
Don Drysdale		29
Bob Gibson		24

The job of the lead-off batter—the first man up in the game—is to start things off by getting on base. The lead-off hitter is usually a fast, steady batter who knows that a base on balls can be as valuable as a hit. But a few lead-off batters can also start the game off with a home-run bang. Bobby Bonds holds the career mark for lead-off home runs and also holds the season record, with 11 lead-off homers in 1973. Bonds may be the greatest player ever in combining power and speed. He's had five seasons with at least 30 home runs and 30 stolen bases. Willie Mays is the only other player with as many as two such seasons.

Most Leadoff Home Runs, Career

Player	Total	Player	Total
Bobby Bonds	35	Bert Campaneris	14
Eddie Yost	28	Frankie Crosetti	14
Jimmy Ryan	22	Pete Rose	14
Lou Brock	21	Bill Bruton	12
Felipe Alou	20	Al Smith	12
Dick McAuliffe	19	Tom Brown	11
Eddie Joost	19	Earle Combs	10
Hank Bauer	18	Johnny Frederick	10
Tommy Harper	16	Harry Hooper	10
Don Buford	15	Wally Moses	10

Two Home Runs in One Inning, AL

Player	Team	Date	Inn.
Ken Williams	STL	Aug 7, 1922	6
Bill Regan	BOS	Jun 16, 1928	4
Joe DiMaggio	NY	Jun 24, 1936	5
Al Kaline	DET	Apr 17, 1955	6
Jim Lemon	WAS	Sep 5, 1959	3
Joe Pepitone	NY	May 23, 1962	8
Rick Reichardt	CAL	Apr 30, 1966	8
Cliff Johnson	NY	Jun 30, 1977	8

Two Home Runs in One Inning, NL

Player	Team	Date	Inn.
Charley Jones	BOS	Jun 10, 1880	8
Bobby Lowe	BOS	May 30, 1894	3
Jake Stenzel	PIT	Jun 6, 1894	3
Hack Wilson	NY	Jul 1, 1925	3
Hank Leiber	NY	Aug 24, 1935	2
Andy Seminick	PHI	Jun 2, 1949	8
Sid Gordon	NY	Jul 31, 1949	2
Willie McCovey	SF	Apr 12, 1973	4
John Boccabella	MON	Jul 6, 1973	6
Lee May	HOU	Apr 29, 1974	6
Andre Dawson	MON	Jul 30, 1978	3
Ray Knight	CIN	May 13, 1980	5

Lou Gehrig, the Iron Horse of the New York Yankees, enjoyed his greatest day on a baseball diamond on June 3, 1932. On that day, Gehrig slugged four home runs in a game against the Philadelphia Athletics, but all "Larrupin' Lou" got for matching one of baseball's toughest records was a brief mention in the newspapers. That same day, John McGraw, the brilliant manager of the New York Giants, stole the headlines by announcing his retirement after 30 years at the helm of the club.

Of the ten men who have hit four homers in one game, only two, Ed Delahanty and Joe Adcock, hit their homers in consecutive at bats. All four of Delahanty's homers were inside-the-park blasts. Adcock came the closest to hitting five home runs in a game. After slamming four at Ebbets Field in Brooklyn on July 31, 1954, he smashed a double high off the left-center-field wall for his fifth hit of the day.

Four Home Runs in One Game, AL

Player	Team	Date	H/A	Cons.	Inns.
Lou Gehrig	NY	Jun 3, 1932	AWAY	NO	9
Pat Seerey	CHI	Jul 18, 1948	AWAY	NO	11
Rocky Colavito	CLE	Jun 10, 1959	AWAY	NO	9

Four Home Runs in One Game, NL

Player	Team	Date	H/A	Cons.	Inns.
Bobby Lowe	BOS	May 30, 1894	HOME	NO	9
Ed Delahanty	PHI	Jul 13, 1896	AWAY	YES	9
Chuck Klein	PHI	Jul 10, 1936	AWAY	NO	10
Gil Hodges	BKN	Aug 31, 1950	HOME	NO	9
Joe Adcock	MIL	Jul 31, 1954	AWAY	YES	9
Willie Mays	SF	Apr 30, 1961	AWAY	NO	9
Mike Schmidt	PHI	Jul 17, 1976	AWAY	NO	10

A switch hitter is a one-man platoon—he can hit either right-handed or left-handed, depending on the pitcher facing him. Why is this so important? When a right-handed pitcher throws a curveball to a right-handed batter, it starts out aimed at his head and then curves down over the plate. The pitcher is counting on the batter's understandable impulse to get out of the way of a ball thrown at his head. But the same pitch poses no threat to a left-handed batter, since he sees it breaking in toward the plate. A switch hitter has the advantage of always seeing the curveball break in toward him.

The greatest switch hitter of them all is Mickey Mantle. He was the first to show that switch hitters could hit for power. Mantle hit 536 home runs in his career, 163 right-handed and 373 left-handed, paving the way for current switch-hitting sluggers like Reggie Smith, Ken Singleton, and Eddie Murray.

Switch-Hit Home Runs in One Game, AL

Player	Team	Date	Player	Team	Date
Johnny Lucadello	STL	Sep 16, 1940	Don Buford	BAL	Apr 9, 1970
Mickey Mantle	NY	May 13, 1955	Roy White	NY	May 7, 1970
	NY	Aug 15, 1955	Reggie Smith	BOS	Jul 2, 1972
	NY	May 18, 1956		BOS	Apr 16, 1973
	NY	Jul 1, 1956	Roy White	NY	Aug 13, 1973
	NY	Jun 12, 1957		NY	Apr 23, 1975
	NY	Jul 28, 1958	Ken Henderson	CHI	Aug 29, 1975
	NY	Sep 15, 1959	Roy White	NY	Aug 3, 1977
	NY	Apr 26, 1961	Eddie Murray	BAL	Jun 13, 1978
	NY	May 6, 1962	Larry Milbourne	SEA	Jul 15, 1978
Tom Tresh	NY	Sep 1, 1963	Willie Wilson	KC	Jun 15, 1979
	NY	Jul 13, 1964	Eddie Murray	BAL	Aug 29, 1979
Mickey Mantle	NY	Aug 12, 1964	U.L. Washington	KC	Sep 21, 1979
Tom Tresh	NY	Jun 6, 1965			
Reggie Smith	BOS	Aug 20, 1967			
	BOS	Aug 11, 1968			

Switch-Hit Home Runs in One Game, NL

Player	Team	Date	Player	Team	Date
Augie Galan	CHI	Jun 25, 1937	Wes Parker	LA	Jun 5, 1966
Jim Russell	BOS	Jun 7, 1948	Pete Rose	CIN	Aug 30, 1966
	BKN	Jul 26, 1950		CIN	Aug 2, 1967
Red Schoendienst	STL	Jul 8, 1951	Ted Simmons	STL	Apr 17, 1975
Maury Wills	LA	May 30, 1962	Reggie Smith	STL	May 4, 1975
Ellis Burton	CHI	Aug 1, 1963		STL	May 22, 1976
	CHI	Sep 7, 1964	Lee Mazzilli	NY	Sep 3, 1978
Jim Lefebvre	LA	May 7, 1966	Ted Simmons	STL	Jun 11, 1979

Smiling as he crosses home plate, **Mickey Mantle** *(opposite page)*, is greeted by Yankee teammates Yogi Berra, Joe Collins, and Hank Bauer *(left to right)* after slamming a home run.

A walk isn't just the result of four bad pitches. Some batters have a good eye and can control the bat well enough to foul off the close pitches. The patient hitters can wait for the pitch they want and accept a walk if they don't get it. They aren't always the best hitters or sluggers, but they do get on base, and that's what counts.

Most Times Walked, Game, AL

Player	Team	Date	BB	Player	Team	Date	BB
Jimmie Foxx	BOS	Jun 16, 1938	6	Earl Averill	CLE	Aug 9, 1932	5
Sammy Strang	CHI	Apr 27, 1902	5	Jo-Jo White	DET	May 18, 1935	5
Elmer Flick	CLE	Jul 18, 1902	5	Lou Gehrig	NY	Aug 27, 1935	5
Kid Elberfeld	DET	Aug 1, 1902	5	Ben Chapman	NY	May 24, 1936	5
Charlie Hemphill	NY	Aug 3, 1911	5	Billy Rogell	DET	Aug 8, 1938	5
Tris Speaker	BOS	Oct 1, 1912	5	Hersh Martin	NY	Sep 1, 1945	5
Roger Peckinpaugh	NY	Jun 2, 1919	5	Larry Doby	CLE	Sep 19, 1951	5
Whitey Witt	NY	Jul 2, 1924	5	Bobby Grich	BAL	Aug 9, 1975	5
Ira Flagstead	BOS	May 8, 1925	5	Roy Smalley	MIN	May 7, 1978	5
Max Bishop	PHI	Apr 29, 1929	5				
	PHI	May 21, 1930	5				

Most Times Walked, Game, NL

Player	Team	Date	BB	Player	Team	Date	BB
Walt Wilmot	CHI	Aug 22, 1891	6	Max West	PIT	Apr 25, 1948	5
Fred Carroll	PIT	Jul 4, 1889	5	Solly Hemus	STL	Sep 15, 1951	5
Pop Smith	BOS	Apr 17, 1890	5	Andy Seminick	PHI	Sep 30, 1951	5
Kip Selbach	CIN	Jun 11, 1899	5	Richie Allen	PHI	Aug 16, 1968	5
Sam Mertes	NY	Aug 12, 1903	5	Ellie Hendricks	CHI	Sep 16, 1972	5
Heinie Groh	NY	May 26, 1922	5	Tim Foli	MON	Sep 7, 1973	5
Hughie Critz	CIN	May 26, 1928	5	Joe Ferguson	HOU	Jun 24, 1978	5
Mel Ott	NY	Oct 5, 1929	5	Johnny Bench	CIN	Jul 22, 1979	5
Gus Suhr	PIT	May 29, 1930	5	Rod Scott	MON	Apr 12, 1980	5
Mel Ott	NY	Sep 1, 1933	5				
	NY	Jun 7, 1943	5				
	NY	Apr 30, 1944	5				

Jimmie Foxx, one of the most feared sluggers in American League history, once drew a record six walks in one game.

BATTING RECORDS

Most Times Struck Out, Game, AL

Player	Team	Date	SO	Inns.
Carl Weilman	STL	Jul 25, 1913	6	15
Rick Reichardt	CAL	May 31, 1966	6	17
Billy Cowan	CAL	Jul 9, 1971	6	20
Cecil Cooper	BOS	Jun 17, 1974	6	15
Donie Bush	DET	May 1, 1910	5	10
Ray Morgan	WAS	1911	5	10
Scott Perry	PHI	Apr 25, 1919	5	11
Ossie Bluege	WAS	Jun 17, 1923	5	11
Lefty Grove	PHI	Jun 10, 1933	5	
Johnny Broaca	NY	Jun 25, 1934	5	
Chet Laabs	DET	Oct 2, 1938	5	
Larry Doby	CLE	Apr 25, 1948	5	
Jim Landis	CHI	Jul 28, 1957	5	
Bob Allison	MIN	Sep 2, 1965	5	
Sandy Valdespino	MIN	Aug 9, 1967	5	20
Ray Jarvis	BOS	Apr 20, 1969	5	
Reggie Jackson	OAK	Sep 27, 1968	5	
Rick Monday	OAK	Apr 29, 1970	5	
Frank Howard	WAS	Sep 19, 1970	5	
Don Buford	BAL	Aug 26, 1971	5	
Bobby Darwin	MIN	May 12, 1972	5	22
Roy Smalley	MIN	Aug 28, 1976	5	17
Rick Manning	CLE	May 15, 1977	5	
Kevin Bell	CHI	Apr 26, 1980	5	

Most Times Struck Out, Game, NL

Player	Team	Date	SO	Inns.
Don Hoak	CHI	May 2, 1956	6	17
Oscar Walker	BUF	Jun 20, 1879	5	
Harry Stovey	BOS	Jun 30, 1891	5	10
Pete Dowling	LOU	Aug 15, 1899	5	
Benny Kauff	NY	May 23, 1918	5	14
Les Bell	STL	May 12, 1927	5	11
Pep Young	PIT	Sep 29, 1935	5	
Dee Fondy	CHI	Jul 22, 1953	5	
Steve Bilko	STL	May 28, 1953	5	10
Jackie Robinson	BKN	Sep 30, 1953	5	10
Bob Sadowski	MIL	Apr 20, 1964	5	
Richie Allen	PHI	Jun 28, 1964	5	
Ron Swoboda	NY	Jun 22, 1969	5	
Steve Whitaker	SF	Apr 14, 1970	5	
Richie Allen	STL	May 24, 1970	5	
Bill Russell	LA	Jun 9, 1971	5	
Pepe Mangual	MON	Aug 11, 1975	5	
Frank Taveras	NY	May 1, 1979	5	

BATTING RECORDS

Most Hits, Game, AL

Player	Team	Date	H	AB	2B	3B	HR	Inns.
Johnny Burnett	CLE	Jul 10, 1932	9	11	2	0	0	18
Rocky Colavito	DET	Jun 24, 1962	7	10	0	1	0	22
Cesar Gutierrez	DET	Jun 21, 1970	7	7	1	0	0	12
Mike Donlin	BAL	Jun 24, 1901	6	6	2	2	0	
Doc Nance	DET	Jul 13, 1901	6	6	1	0	0	
Erwin Harvey	CLE	Apr 25, 1902	6	6	0	0	0	
Danny Murphy	PHI	Jul 8, 1902	6	6	0	0	1	
Jimmy Williams	BAL	Aug 25, 1902	6	6	1	1	0	
Bobby Veach	DET	Sep 17, 1920	6	6	1	1	1	12
George Sisler	STL	Aug 9, 1921	6	9	0	1	0	19
Frank Brower	CLE	Aug 7, 1923	6	6	1	0	0	
George Burns	CLE	Jun 19, 1924	6	6	3	1	0	
Ty Cobb	DET	May 5, 1925	6	6	1	0	3	
Jimmie Foxx	PHI	May 30, 1930	6	7	2	1	0	
Doc Cramer	PHI	Jun 20, 1932	6	6	0	0	0	
Jimmie Foxx	PHI	Jul 10, 1932	6	9	1	0	3	18
Sammy West	STL	Apr 13, 1933	6	6	1	0	0	11
Myril Hoag	NY	Jun 6, 1934	6	6	0	0	0	
Bob Johnson	PHI	Jun 16, 1934	6	6	1	0	2	11
Doc Cramer	PHI	Jul 13, 1935	6	6	1	0	0	
Bruce Campbell	CLE	Jul 2, 1936	6	6	1	0	0	
Rip Radcliff	CHI	Jul 18, 1936	6	7	2	0	0	
Hank Steinbacher	CHI	Jun 22, 1938	6	6	1	0	0	
George Myatt	WAS	May 1, 1944	6	6	1	0	0	
Stan Spence	WAS	Jun 1, 1944	6	6	0	0	1	
George Kell	DET	Sep 20, 1946	6	7	1	0	0	
Jim Fridley	CLE	Apr 29, 1952	6	6	0	0	0	
Jimmy Piersall	BOS	Jun 10, 1953	6	6	1	0	0	
Joe DeMaestri	KC	Jul 8, 1955	6	6	0	0	0	11
Pete Runnels	BOS	Aug 30, 1960	6	7	1	0	0	
Floyd Robinson	CHI	Jul 22, 1962	6	6	0	0	0	
Bob Oliver	KC	May 4, 1969	6	6	1	0	1	
Jim Northrup	DET	Aug 28, 1969	6	6	0	0	2	13
John Briggs	MIL	Aug 4, 1973	6	6	2	0	0	
Jorge Orta	CLE	Jun 15, 1980	6	6	1	0	0	

The Early Years:
1901–1919

Baseball as we know it today began when the American League was established in 1901. To get players for their teams, the new AL clubs offered higher pay to players from the twenty-five-year-old National League. This raiding continued until the two rival leagues signed a peace treaty in 1903 that recognized the American League as the second major league. Later that year the champion team from each league played in the first World Series.

The early years of baseball are called the dead-ball era. The "dead ball" was heavier and slower than the ball used today, and it didn't travel far when hit. This made baseball more of a defensive struggle than it is today. Home runs were rare: It took just six homers for Tommy Leach to lead the National League in 1902.

Each team had only a few pitchers, and they were expected to play the whole game. Jack Chesbro of the New York Highlanders (later Yankees) won 41 games in 1904 and completed 48 of the 51 games he started. Today, few pitchers even start 40 games in a season.

One pennant race in the early years is remembered for a famous mistake. The 1908 New York Giants were forced into a one-game play-off with the Chicago Cubs because of a base-running error by rookie Fred Merkle. The score was tied and the winning run on third base in the last of the ninth. Up came Al Bridwell, who singled and drove home the winning run. Merkle, the runner on first, left the field without touching second base. Cub second baseman Johnny Evers noticed this error, retrieved the ball from the outfield, and stepped on second, forcing out the embarrassed Merkle and erasing the run. The Cubs beat the Giants in the replay of that game to win the pennant.

The year 1919 proved an important turning point in baseball history. The Cincinnati Reds upset the powerful Chicago White Sox in an eight-game World Series, surprising fans by scoring easily against Chicago's ace pitchers. Eight members of the Chicago team, including star outfielder Joe Jackson and two of their starting pitchers, were accused of trying to lose the Series in exchange for bribes from gamblers. A jury found the players not guilty, but Judge Kenesaw Mountain Landis, the newly appointed Commissioner of Baseball, moved to protect the major leagues from any hint of dishonesty by barring the eight players from organized baseball for life. The team involved in the only major scandal in baseball history has become known as "the Black Sox."

Another major change was signaled in 1919 when a Boston Red Sox pitcher-turned-outfielder named George Herman "Babe" Ruth hit 29 home runs—more than the home run total of ten whole *teams*—to set a major league record. With powerful hitting like this, pitching would no longer dominate the game as it once had. Unfortunately for Red Sox fans, their owner was short of cash and sold Ruth to the Yankees during the off-season. The sale marked the start of a long string of great Yankee teams and a new era in baseball history.

WORLD SERIES

New Yorkers lined up outside the Polo Grounds, home of the Giants, to watch the 1912 World Series *(top)*. The Giants lost the Series to the Boston Red Sox. They were also beaten in 1911 and 1913 by Connie Mack's Philadelphia Athletics, a team led by Stuffy McInnis, Danny Murphy, Frank "Home Run" Baker, Jack Barry, and Eddie Collins *(bottom, left to right)*. McInnis, Collins, Barry, and Baker were called "The $100,000 Infield." That sum of $100,000, a fortune in those days, is a fraction of what these four would be paid in today's free agent market.

OLD-TIME HITTING STARS

Honus Wagner of the Pirates *(top left)* is considered the greatest shortstop of all time. A fine hitter, fielder, and base-runner, he is said to have been the best all-around player ever by the men who played with and against him. Tris Speaker played centerfield for the Boston Red Sox and Cleveland Indians for twenty-two years *(top right)*. Although he won only one batting title, his lifetime average of .344 ranks seventh in baseball history. Joe Jackson's talents as a hitter have been overshadowed by his part in the Black Sox scandal, when he was tried for purposely losing the 1919 World Series. A well-liked player, "Shoeless Joe" *(bottom right)* was stopped by a newsboy outside the courthouse who looked up at him with tears in his eyes and pleaded, "Say it ain't so, Joe!"

CHRISTY MATHEWSON

Tall and good-looking, Christy Mathewson came off the campus of Bucknell University to become a star pitcher for the New York Giants and one of the most popular and respected players of the day *(top)*. An outstanding control pitcher, "Matty" threw a pitch called his fadeaway—now known as a screwball—with remarkable accuracy, walking just over one-and-a-half batters per game during his 17-year career. In the 1905 World Series against the Philadelphia Athletics, he won three complete-game shutouts, a feat that has never been equaled. He ended his career in Cincinnati, as the manager of the Reds *(left)*.

WALTER JOHNSON

Walter Johnson, like Christy Mathewson, was known as much for his gentlemanly behavior off the field as for his great talent on the mound. Johnson threw one pitch—a blazing fastball timed at just under 100 miles per hour. He threw it well enough to strike out a record 3,508 batters and to post a total of 113 shutouts, also a record. "The Big Train" won 416 games in his 21 years with the Washington Senators, one of the American League's worst teams during much of his career. He won 20 or more games for ten straight years, from 1910 to 1919, averaging 26 wins a year during that stretch.

THE GEORGIA PEACH

Ty Cobb was the greatest hitter for average ever, and one of the fiercest competitors to play the game. Cobb was among the most hated players of his time; he wanted to win so much that he wouldn't hesitate to knock down an opponent if it would help his Tigers team. His determination and talent are reflected in his lifetime batting records: he ranks first in hits, runs, and batting average; second in total games played, at bats, triples, and stolen bases; third in doubles; and fourth in runs batted in. Cobb topped the .300 mark in twenty-three consecutive seasons, and his career batting average of .367 will surely never be topped.

BATTING RECORDS

Most Hits, Game, NL

Player	Team	Date	H	AB	2B	3B	HR	Inns.
Wilbert Robinson	BAL	Jun 10, 1892	7	7	1	0	0	
Rennie Stennett	PIT	Sep 16, 1975	7	7	2	1	0	
Davy Force	PHI	Jun 27, 1876	6	6	1	0	0	
Cal McVey	CHI	Jul 22, 1876	6	7	1	0	0	
	CHI	Jul 25, 1876	6	7	1	0	0	
Ross Barnes	CHI	Jul 27, 1876	6	6	1	1	0	
Paul Hines	PRO	Aug 26, 1879	6	6	0	0	0	10
George Gore	CHI	May 7, 1880	6	6	0	0	0	
Buttercup Dickerson	WOR	Jun 16, 1881	6	6	0	1	0	
Sam Wise	BOS	Jun 20, 1883	6	7	1	1	0	
Dan Brouthers	BUF	Jul 19, 1883	6	6	2	0	0	
Danny Richardson	NY	Jun 11, 1887	6	7	0	0	0	
King Kelly	BOS	Aug 27, 1887	6	7	1	0	1	
Jerry Denny	IND	May 4, 1889	6	6	1	0	1	
Larry Twitchell	CLE	Aug 15, 1889	6	6	1	3	1	
Jack Glasscock	NY	Sep 27, 1890	6	6	0	0	0	
Bobby Lowe	BOS	Jun 11, 1891	6	6	1	0	1	
Henry Larkin	WAS	Jun 7, 1892	6	7	0	1	0	
Jack Boyle	PHI	Jul 6, 1893	6	6	1	0	0	11
Duff Cooley	STL	Sep 30, 1893	6	6	1	0	0	
Ed Delahanty	PHI	Jun 16, 1894	6	6	1	0	0	
Steve Brodie	BAL	Jul 9, 1894	6	6	2	1	0	
Chief Zimmer	CLE	Jul 11, 1894	6	6	2	0	0	10
Sam Thompson	PHI	Aug 17, 1894	6	7	1	1	0	
Roger Connor	STL	Jun 1, 1895	6	6	2	1	0	
George Davis	NY	Aug 15, 1895	6	6	2	1	0	
Jake Stenzel	PIT	May 14, 1896	6	6	0	0	0	
Fred Tenney	BOS	May 31, 1897	6	8	1	0	0	
Dick Harley	STL	Jun 24, 1897	6	6	1	0	0	12
Barry McCormick	CHI	Jun 29, 1897	6	8	0	1	1	
Tommy Tucker	WAS	Jul 15, 1897	6	6	1	0	0	
Willie Keeler	BAL	Sep 3, 1897	6	6	0	1	0	
Jack Doyle	BAL	Sep 3, 1897	6	6	2	0	0	
Chick Stahl	BOS	May 31, 1899	6	6	0	0	0	
Ginger Beaumont	PIT	Jul 22, 1899	6	6	0	0	0	
Kip Selbach	NY	Jun 9, 1901	6	7	2	0	0	
George Cutshaw	BKN	Aug 9, 1915	6	6	0	0	0	
Carson Bigbee	PIT	Aug 22, 1917	6	11	0	0	0	22
Dave Bancroft	NY	Jun 28, 1920	6	6	0	0	0	
Johnny Gooch	PIT	Jul 7, 1922	6	8	1	0	0	18
Max Carey	PIT	Jul 7, 1922	6	6	1	0	0	18
Jack Fournier	BKN	Jun 29, 1923	6	6	2	0	1	
Kiki Cuyler	PIT	Aug 9, 1924	6	6	3	1	0	
Frankie Frisch	NY	Sep 10, 1924	6	7	0	0	1	
Jim Bottomley	STL	Sep 16, 1924	6	6	1	0	2	
Paul Waner	PIT	Aug 26, 1926	6	6	2	1	0	
Lloyd Waner	PIT	Jun 15, 1929	6	8	1	1	0	14
Hank DeBerry	BKN	Jun 23, 1929	6	7	0	0	0	14
Wally Gilbert	BKN	May 30, 1931	6	7	1	0	0	

Before moving on to a 17-year career as the Brooklyn manager, **Wilbert Robinson** was the first player to belt 7 hits in one game, a record matched just once in NL history.

Most Hits, Game, NL (continued)

Player	Team	Date	H	AB	2B	3B	HR	Inns.
Jim Bottomley	STL	Aug 5, 1931	6	6	1	0	0	
Tony Cuccinello	CIN	Aug 13, 1931	6	6	2	1	0	
Terry Moore	STL	Sep 5, 1935	6	6	1	0	0	
Ernie Lombardi	CIN	May 9, 1937	6	6	1	0	0	
Frank Demaree	CHI	Jul 5, 1937	6	7	2	0	0	14
Cookie Lavagetto	BKN	Sep 23, 1939	6	6	1	1	0	
Walker Cooper	CIN	Jul 6, 1949	6	7	0	0	3	
Johnny Hopp	PIT	May 14, 1950	6	6	0	0	2	
Connie Ryan	PHI	Apr 16, 1953	6	6	2	0	0	
Dick Groat	PIT	May 13, 1960	6	6	3	0	0	
Jesus Alou	SF	Jul 10, 1964	6	6	0	0	1	
Joe Morgan	HOU	Jul 8, 1965	6	6	0	1	2	12
Felix Millan	ATL	Jul 6, 1970	6	6	1	1	0	
Don Kessinger	CHI	Jul 17, 1971	6	6	1	0	0	10
Willie Davis	LA	May 24, 1973	6	9	0	0	0	19
Bill Madlock	CHI	Jul 26, 1975	6	6	0	1	0	10
Jose Cardenal	CHI	May 2, 1976	6	7	1	0	1	14
Gene Richards	SD	Jul 26, 1977	6	7	1	0	0	15

BATTING RECORDS

Most Combined Hits and Walks, Season, AL

Player	Team		H	BB	Total
Babe Ruth	NY	1923	205	170	375
Ted Williams	BOS	1949	194	162	356
Babe Ruth	NY	1921	204	144	348
Ted Williams	BOS	1947	181	162	343
Babe Ruth	NY	1924	200	142	342
Lou Gehrig	NY	1936	205	130	335
Ted Williams	BOS	1946	176	156	332
	BOS	1942	186	145	331
Babe Ruth	NY	1927	192	138	330
Ted Williams	BOS	1941	185	145	330
Jimmie Foxx	PHI	1932	213	116	329
Babe Ruth	NY	1926	184	144	328
Lou Gehrig	NY	1931	211	117	328
	NY	1927	218	109	327
Babe Ruth	NY	1931	199	128	327
Lou Gehrig	NY	1937	200	127	327
Ty Cobb	DET	1915	208	118	326
Babe Ruth	NY	1930	186	136	322
Lou Gehrig	NY	1930	220	101	321
Babe Ruth	NY	1920	172	148	320
Lou Gehrig	NY	1934	210	109	319
Mickey Mantle	NY	1957	173	146	319
Norm Cash	DET	1961	193	124	317
Lou Gehrig	NY	1932	208	108	316
Jimmie Foxx	BOS	1938	197	116	316
Ted Williams	BOS	1948	188	126	314
Carl Yastrzemski	BOS	1970	186	128	314
Charlie Gehringer	DET	1934	214	99	313
Ted Williams	BOS	1951	169	144	313
Tris Speaker	CLE	1920	214	97	311
	CLE	1923	218	93	311
Buddy Myer	WAS	1935	215	96	311
Charlie Gehringer	DET	1936	227	83	310
Eddie Yost	WAS	1950	169	141	310

Most Combined Hits and Walks, Season, NL

Player	Team		H	BB	Total
Billy Hamilton	PHI	1894	220	126	346
Lefty O'Doul	PHI	1929	254	76	330
Rogers Hornsby	STL	1924	227	89	316
	CHI	1929	229	87	316
	STL	1922	250	65	315
Woody English	CHI	1930	214	100	314
Stan Musial	STL	1949	207	107	314
Hack Wilson	CHI	1930	208	105	313
Richie Ashburn	PHI	1958	215	97	312
Bill Terry	NY	1930	254	57	311

Nothing kills a rally like a double play—two outs in one swing, with men on base. One of the most overlooked qualities in a ballplayer is the speed to keep the other team from doubling him up at first. It's important to be fast, but it also helps to be a left-handed hitter—it takes two extra steps to get to first from the right side of the plate, and those two steps can make a big difference..

Hardest to Double Up, Career

Player	AB	DP	Ratio
Don Buford	4553	33	138
Don Blasingame	5296	43	123
Mickey Rivers	4540	38	119
Richie Ashburn	8365	85	98
Joe Morgan	7737	80	97
George Case	3964	42	94
Vic Davalillo	4017	43	93
Lou Brock	10332	14	91
Stan Hack	7100	78	91
Bill Nicholson	5534	61	91
Bud Harrelson	4744	53	90
Arky Vaughan	6125	70	88
Rick Monday	5571	65	86
Del Unser	5142	60	86
Bert Campaneris	8459	102	83
Bill Bruton	6065	73	83
Augie Galan	5937	72	82
Maury Wills	7588	92	82
Sandy Alomar	4780	58	82
Dick McAuliffe	6185	77	80

Oriole outfielder and lead-off man **Don Buford,** who hit into just one double play for every 138 at bats.

Do home-run hitters strike out more than other hitters? This table certainly indicates that they do. The leaders, Dave Nicholson, Dave Kingman, Richie Allen, Mike Schmidt, and Reggie Jackson, are all big men who take big swings and hit the ball a very long way—when they connect. The hardest men to strike out are the players who choke up on the bat and just try to make contact. The five easiest men to strike out averaged 25 homers a year; the five hardest to strike out averaged just 3.

Hardest to Strike Out, Career

Player	Yrs.	AB	SO	Ratio
Joe Sewell	14	7132	114	62.6
Lloyd Waner	18	7772	173	44.9
Nellie Fox	19	9232	216	42.7
Tommy Holmes	11	4992	122	40.9
Andy High	13	4400	130	33.8
Sam Rice	20	9269	275	33.7
Frankie Frisch	19	9112	272	33.5
Don Mueller	12	4364	146	29.9

Easiest to Strike Out, Career

Player	Yrs.	AB	SO	Ratio
Dave Nicholson	7	1419	573	2.48
Dave Kingman	10	3839	1139	3.37
Mike Schmidt	9	4261	1077	3.96
Reggie Jackson	14	6863	1728	3.97
Bobby Bonds	13	6880	1713	4.02
Richie Allen	15	6332	1556	4.07
Donn Clendenon	12	4648	1140	4.08
Rick Monday	15	5572	1362	4.09
Willie Stargell	19	7794	1903	4.10
Woodie Held	14	4019	944	4.25
Frank Howard	16	6488	1460	4.44
Deron Johnson	15	5940	1318	4.51
Jimmy Wynn	16	6653	1427	4.66
Mickey Mantle	18	8102	1710	4.73
Harmon Killebrew	22	8147	1699	4.80
Lee May	16	7463	1538	4.85
Bob Allison	13	5032	1033	4.87
Doug Rader	11	5186	1057	4.90
Wally Post	15	4007	813	4.92
Tony Perez	17	8503	1628	5.22
George Scott	14	7433	1418	5.24
Larry Doby	13	5348	1011	5.29
Willie McCovey	22	8197	1550	5.29
Boog Powell	17	6681	1226	5.45
Eddie Mathews	17	8537	1487	5.74
Lou Brock	19	10332	1730	5.97

One of baseball's most extraordinary feats is the winning of a Triple Crown, when a batter leads his league in home runs, runs batted in, and batting average in the same year. Only twelve players have ever won this Triple Crown, and only Ted Williams and Rogers Hornsby have done it twice.

Even if you're a power hitter who can hit for a high batting average, there's no guarantee that you'll achieve a Triple Crown. Babe Ruth had a lifetime batting average of .342 and hit as high as .393, but he could never put together a Triple Crown season. The one time he led his league in batting he fell eight RBIs short. Ruth is in good company, though; Honus Wagner, Willie Mays, Joe DiMaggio, Stan Musial, Hank Greenberg, Henry Aaron, and Roberto Clemente were all great hitters noted for strength and consistency, but none ever achieved this rare distinction.

Napoleon "Nap" Lajoie won the Triple Crown in 1901. He led the American League in batting by a whopping 81 points, hitting .422 to runnner-up Mike Donlin's .341.

BATTING RECORDS

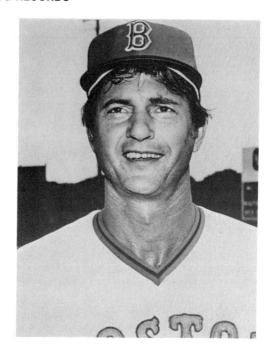

Carl Yastrzemski's Triple Crown season in 1967 almost single-handedly brought the Red Sox the AL pennant. In the last two weeks of the season, "Yaz" had 23 hits in 44 at bats—a .523 average!

Triple Crown Winners, AL

Player	Team		HR	RBI	BA
Nap Lajoie	PHI	1901	14	125	.422
Ty Cobb	DET	1909	9	115	.377
Jimmie Foxx	PHI	1933	48	163	.356
Lou Gehrig	NY	1934	49	165	.363
Ted Williams	BOS	1942	36	137	.356
	BOS	1947	32	114	.343
Mickey Mantle	NY	1956	52	130	.353
Frank Robinson	BAL	1966	49	122	.316
Carl Yastrzemski	BOS	1967	44	121	.326

Triple Crown Winners, NL

Player	Team		HR	RBI	BA
Paul Hines	PRO	1878	4	50	.358
Hugh Duffy	BOS	1894	18	145	.438
Heinie Zimmerman	CHI	1912	14	103	.372
Rogers Hornsby	STL	1922	42	152	.401
	STL	1925	39	143	.403
Chuck Klein	PHI	1933	28	120	.368
Joe Medwick	STL	1937	31	154	.374

Ever since Ted Williams hit .406 in 1941, the question has been asked, "Will there ever be another .400 hitter?" The player who has come closest since then is George Brett, with his .390 batting average in 1980.

The odds are heavily against another .400 hitter because of the tremendous improvement in relief pitching and fielding. Today's players also face the additional handicaps of a longer schedule, which wears down even the strongest players, and more night games, in which the ball is harder to see.

It's worth noting that all but two of the .400 hitters were under 30 years old. The exceptions are Ty Cobb, 35 when he hit .401 in 1922, and Bill Terry, who was 31 when he hit .401 in 1930.

The unluckiest .400 hitters were Joe Jackson in 1911 and Cobb in 1922. Each cracked the magic .400 mark but didn't lead their leagues in batting.

St. Louis Browns first baseman **George Sisler** *(opposite page),* one of the game's greatest hitters, topped the .400 mark in 1920 and 1922. He set the all-time season record of 257 hits in 1920. **Ted Williams** *(right)* was known for his great eye at the plate, rarely swinging at a bad pitch. When he hit .406 in 1941, he drew enough walks to notch an incredible on-base percentage of .551.

The .400 Hitters, AL

Player	Team		G	AB	H	2B	3B	HR	R	RBI	BA
Nap Lajoie	PHI	1901	131	543	229	48	14	14	146	125	.422
Ty Cobb	DET	1911	146	591	248	47	24	8	147	144	.420
George Sisler	STL	1922	142	586	246	52	18	8	134	105	.420
Ty Cobb	DET	1912	140	553	227	30	23	7	119	90	.410
Joe Jackson	CLE	1911	147	571	233	43	19	7	126	83	.408
George Sisler	STL	1920	154	631	257	49	18	19	136	122	.407
Ted Williams	BOS	1941	143	456	185	33	3	37	135	120	.406
Harry Heilmann	DET	1923	144	524	211	44	11	18	121	115	.403
Ty Cobb	DET	1922	137	526	211	42	16	4	99	99	.401

The .400 Hitters, NL

Player	Team		G	AB	H	2B	3B	HR	R	RBI	BA
Hugh Duffy	BOS	1894	124	539	236	50	13	18	160	145	.438
Willie Keeler	BAL	1897	128	562	243	27	19	1	147	74	.432
Rogers Hornsby	STL	1924	143	536	227	43	14	25	121	94	.424
Jesse Burkett	CLE	1895	132	555	235	21	15	5	149	83	.423
	CLE	1896	133	585	240	26	16	6	159	72	.410
Ed Delahanty	PHI	1899	145	573	234	56	9	9	123	137	.408
Fred Clarke	LOU	1897	129	525	213	28	15	6	122	67	.406
Sam Thompson	PHI	1894	102	458	185	29	27	13	115	141	.404
Rogers Hornsby	STL	1925	138	504	203	41	10	39	123	143	.403
Jesse Burkett	STL	1899	138	567	228	17	10	7	115	71	.402
Rogers Hornsby	STL	1922	154	623	250	46	14	42	141	152	.401
Bill Terry	NY	1930	154	633	254	39	15	23	139	129	.401
Ed Delahanty	PHI	1894	114	497	199	36	16	4	149	131	.400

Fans keep talking about how strong major league pitching has become and how today's hitters aren't what they used to be. But the fact is that in the 1970s, seven players entered the coveted 3,000-hit circle—almost as many as in the history of baseball up to 1970.

Ty Cobb, the youngest to top 3,000 hits, made it at age 34, in his 17th season. Pete Rose, however, reached the mark in his 16th season, and is considered the only active player with a chance at breaking Cobb's lifetime mark.

Some of the game's greatest hitters did not make 3,000 hits. Babe Ruth probably would have if he hadn't spent several seasons as a pitcher, playing just once every four days. He retired with 2,873. Ted Williams spent more than four years in the armed forces and finished with 2,654 hits. The man who came closest was Sam Rice, who ended his career with 2,987 hits, just 13 shy of 3,000.

The 3,000-Hit Club

Player	Yrs.	G	AB	H	BA
Ty Cobb	24	3033	11429	4191	.367
Hank Aaron	23	3298	12364	3771	.305
Stan Musial	22	3026	10972	3630	.331
Pete Rose	18	2830	11479	3557	.310
Tris Speaker	22	2789	10208	3515	.344
Honus Wagner	21	2789	10449	3430	.328
Eddie Collins	25	2826	9949	3311	.333
Willie Mays	22	2992	10881	3283	.302
Nap Lajoie	21	2481	9599	3251	.339
Paul Waner	20	2549	9459	3152	.333
Carl Yastrzemski	20	2967	10811	3109	.288
Cap Anson	22	2276	9120	3041	.333
Lou Brock	19	2616	10332	3023	.293
Al Kaline	22	2834	10116	3007	.297
Roberto Clemente	18	2433	9454	3000	.317

Highest Batting Average, Career

Player	BA	Player	BA
Ty Cobb	.367	Bill Terry	.341
Rogers Hornsby	.358	Jesse Burkett	.340
Joe Jackson	.356	George Sisler	.340
Ed Delahanty	.346	Lou Gehrig	.340
Willie Keeler	.345	Nap Lajoie	.339
Ted Williams	.344	Riggs Stephenson	.336
Tris Speaker	.344	Al Simmons	.334
Billy Hamilton	.344	Rod Carew	.333
Dan Brouthers	.343	Cap Anson	.333
Pete Browning	.343	Paul Waner	.333
Babe Ruth	.342	Eddie Collins	.333
Harry Heilmann	.342		

Ty Cobb of the Detroit Tigers is one of baseball's legendary hitters. In 1960, former outfielder Lefty O'Doul was asked how Cobb would hit with the modern, lively baseball. "About .340," O'Doul responded. Why such a low batting average? "Well," he said, " you have to take into consideration the man is now seventy-three years old!"

RUNS AND RUNS BATTED IN

Who is more important, the man who scores a run or the man who drives the run in? The question has no real answer; it's like asking a football fan whether the man who throws a touchdown pass is more important than the man who catches it.

Yet for some reason, baseball fans tend to glorify the man who gets the RBI and ignore the scorer. A player with a great many RBIs must hit well with men on base, but he must also have teammates who get on base ahead of him. Hack Wilson and Chuck Klein drove in 190 and 170 runs, respectively, in 1930. It's no coincidence that these totals, the two highest in NL history, came in a year when the National League had an overall batting average of .303. You can't set an RBI record if your teammates aren't hitting and getting on base.

On the other hand, a runner can put himself in position to score runs by stealing bases, stretching a single into a double, or tagging up on fly balls. A fast, smart base-runner is worth a bushel of runs to his team and many RBIs for the men who follow him in the line-up. Of course, no matter how often you put yourself in position to score on a single, you won't score if your teammates don't come through with that hit.

So even though RBI and run records represent great accomplishments by individuals, they also tell a lot about the hitting ability of the teams they played on.

Tommy Harper scores on a steal of home to climax a dramatic run around the bases in a 1974 Boston-Baltimore game. Harper first doubled, then stole third and home, showing how a great base-runner can make a run without any help from his teammates.

BATTING RECORDS

Most Runs, Season, AL

Player	Team		R
Babe Ruth	NY	1921	177
Lou Gehrig	NY	1936	167
Babe Ruth	NY	1928	163
Lou Gehrig	NY	1931	163
Babe Ruth	NY	1920	158
	NY	1927	158
Al Simmons	PHI	1930	152
Babe Ruth	NY	1923	151
Jimmie Foxx	PHI	1932	151
Joe DiMaggio	NY	1937	151

Most Runs, Season, NL

Player	Team		R
Billy Hamilton	PHI	1894	192
Joe Kelley	BAL	1894	167
Billy Hamilton	PHI	1895	166
Willie Keeler	BAL	1894	165
	BAL	1895	162
Hugh Duffy	BOS	1894	160
Jesse Burkett	CLE	1896	160
Hughie Jennings	BAL	1895	159
Bobby Lowe	BOS	1894	158
Chuck Klein	PHI	1930	158

Most Runs, Career

Player	R
Ty Cobb	2244
Babe Ruth	2174
Hank Aaron	2174
Willie Mays	2062
Stan Musial	1949
Lou Gehrig	1888
Tris Speaker	1881
Mel Ott	1859
Pete Rose	1842
Frank Robinson	1829
Eddie Collins	1818
Ted Williams	1798
Charlie Gehringer	1774
Jimmie Foxx	1751
Honus Wagner	1740
Willie Keeler	1720
Cap Anson	1719
Jesse Burkett	1716
Billy Hamilton	1689
Carl Yastrzemski	1689

BATTING RECORDS

Most RBIs, Season, AL

Player	Team		RBI
Lou Gehrig	NY	1931	184
Hank Greenberg	DET	1937	183
Jimmie Foxx	BOS	1938	175
Lou Gehrig	NY	1927	175
	NY	1930	174
Babe Ruth	NY	1921	171
Hank Greenberg	DET	1935	170
Jimmie Foxx	PHI	1932	169
Joe DiMaggio	NY	1937	167
Al Simmons	PHI	1930	165
Lou Gehrig	NY	1934	165

Most RBIs, Season, NL

Player	Team		RBI
Hack Wilson	CHI	1930	190
Chuck Klein	PHI	1930	170
Sam Thompson	DET	1887	166
	PHI	1895	165
Hack Wilson	CHI	1929	159
Joe Medwick	STL	1937	154
Tommy Davis	LA	1962	153
Rogers Hornsby	STL	1922	152
Mel Ott	NY	1929	151
Rogers Hornsby	CHI	1929	149
George Foster	CIN	1977	149

Most RBIs, Career

Player	RBI
Hank Aaron	2297
Babe Ruth	2204
Lou Gehrig	1991
Ty Cobb	1959
Stan Musial	1951
Jimmie Foxx	1922
Willie Mays	1903
Mel Ott	1860
Ted Williams	1839
Al Simmons	1827
Frank Robinson	1812
Honus Wagner	1732
Cap Anson	1715
Carl Yastrzemski	1663
Ernie Banks	1636
Goose Goslin	1609
Nap Lajoie	1599
Rogers Hornsby	1596
Harmon Killebrew	1584
Al Kaline	1583

Hack Wilson, early in his career, with the New York Giants.

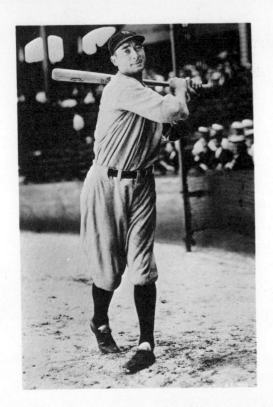

The Yankee second baseman "Poosh 'Em Up" **Tony Lazzeri** drove in an AL-record 11 runs in one game in 1936.

Most RBIs, Game, AL

Player	Team	Date	RBI
Tony Lazzeri	NY	May 24, 1936	11
Rudy York	BOS	Jul 27, 1946	10
Norm Zauchin	BOS	May 27, 1955	10
Reggie Jackson	OAK	Jun 14, 1969	10
Fred Lynn	BOS	Jun 18, 1975	10
Jimmie Foxx	PHI	Aug 14, 1933	9
Jim Tabor	BOS	Jul 4, 1939	9
Jackie Jensen	BOS	Aug 2, 1956	9
Jim Gentile	BAL	May 9, 1961	9

Most RBIs, Game, NL

Player	Team	Date	RBI
Jim Bottomley	STL	Sep 16, 1924	12
Wilbert Robinson	BAL	Jun 10, 1892	11
Phil Weintraub	NY	Apr 30, 1944	11
Walker Cooper	NY	Jul 6, 1949	10
Russ Wrightstone	PHI	Jun 11, 1926	9
Johnny Rizzo	PIT	May 30, 1939	9
Gil Hodges	BKN	Aug 31, 1950	9
Smoky Burgess	CIN	Jul 29, 1955	9
Tony Cloninger	ATL	Jul 3, 1966	9

BATTING RECORDS

More RBIs than Games Played, Season, AL

Player	Team		RBI	G	Diff.
Lou Gehrig	NY	1931	184	155	29
Hank Greenberg	DET	1937	183	154	29
Al Simmons	PHI	1930	165	138	27
Jimmie Foxx	BOS	1938	175	149	26
Lou Gehrig	NY	1927	175	155	20
	NY	1930	174	154	20
Babe Ruth	NY	1921	171	152	19
	NY	1929	154	135	19
	NY	1931	153	145	18
Hank Greenberg	DET	1935	170	152	18
Joe DiMaggio	NY	1937	167	151	16
Jimmie Foxx	PHI	1932	169	154	15
Al Simmons	PHI	1928	157	143	14
Jimmie Foxx	PHI	1933	163	149	14
Babe Ruth	NY	1927	164	151	13
Lou Gehrig	NY	1934	165	154	11
Hal Trosky	CLE	1936	162	151	11
Babe Ruth	NY	1930	153	145	8
Walt Dropo	BOS	1950	144	136	8
Joe DiMaggio	NY	1939	126	120	6
Babe Ruth	NY	1932	137	133	4
Vern Stephens	BOS	1949	159	155	4
Ted Williams	BOS	1949	159	155	4
Ken Williams	STL	1925	105	102	3
Jimmie Foxx	PHI	1930	156	153	3
Ken Williams	STL	1922	155	153	2
Al Simmons	PHI	1927	108	106	2
Lou Gehrig	NY	1937	159	157	2
Hank Greenberg	DET	1940	150	148	2
Joe DiMaggio	NY	1948	155	153	2
	NY	1940	133	132	1
George Brett	KC	1980	118	117	1

More RBIs than Games Played, Season, NL

Player	Team		RBI	G	Diff.
Hack Wilson	CHI	1930	190	155	35
Chuck Klein	PHI	1930	170	156	14
Hack Wilson	CHI	1929	159	150	9
Rogers Hornsby	STL	1925	143	138	5
Mel Ott	NY	1929	151	150	1

The 1980 season was the year of the runner, with a record total of 3,294 stolen bases, 1,839 in the National League and 1,455 in the American. A record eight players stole 60 or more bases. Oakland's Rickey Henderson broke Ty Cobb's 65-year-old AL record with an even 100 steals, and Ron LeFlore's 97 made him the only man ever to lead both leagues in steals. LeFlore and his Montreal teammate Rodney Scott combined for 160 steals, the highest ever by two teammates. San Diego became the first team ever with three players to steal over 50 bases—Gene Richards (61), Ozzie Smith (57), and Jerry Mumphrey (52).

Most Stolen Bases, Season, AL

Player	Team		SB	Player	Team		SB
Rickey Henderson	OAK	1980	100	Mickey Rivers	CAL	1975	70
Ty Cobb	DET	1915	96	Ty Cobb	DET	1916	68
Clyde Milan	WAS	1912	88	Ron LeFlore	DET	1978	68
Ty Cobb	DET	1911	83	Eddie Collins	PHI	1909	67
Willie Wilson	KC	1979	83	Ty Cobb	DET	1910	65
Eddie Collins	PHI	1910	81	Eddie Collins	PHI	1912	63
Ron LeFlore	DET	1979	79	Sam Rice	WAS	1920	63
Willie Wilson	KC	1980	79	Miguel Dilone	CLE	1980	63
Ty Cobb	DET	1909	76	Danny Moeller	WAS	1913	62
Clyde Milan	WAS	1913	75	Bert Campaneris	OAK	1968	62
Billy North	OAK	1976	75	Ty Cobb	DET	1912	61
Fritz Maisel	NY	1914	74	Ben Chapman	NY	1931	61
Tommy Harper	SEA	1969	73	George Case	WAS	1943	60

Most Stolen Bases, Season, NL

Player	Team		SB	Player	Team		SB
Lou Brock	STL	1974	118	Bob Bescher	CIN	1912	67
Maury Wills	LA	1962	104	Joe Morgan	CIN	1973	67
Ron LeFlore	MON	1980	97		CIN	1975	67
Omar Moreno	PIT	1980	96	Lou Brock	STL	1971	64
Bob Bescher	CIN	1911	83	Max Carey	PIT	1916	63
Maury Wills	LA	1965	83	Lou Brock	STL	1972	63
Dave Collins	CIN	1980	79	Dave Lopes	LA	1976	63
Dave Lopes	LA	1975	77	Rod Scott	MON	1980	63
Omar Moreno	PIT	1979	77	George Burns	NY	1914	62
Lou Brock	STL	1966	74	Lou Brock	STL	1968	62
Omar Moreno	PIT	1978	71	Honus Wagner	PIT	1907	61
Bob Bescher	CIN	1910	70	Josh Devore	NY	1911	61
Lou Brock	STL	1973	70	Max Carey	PIT	1913	61
Frank Taveras	PIT	1977	70	Cesar Cedeno	HOU	1977	61
Frank Chance	CHI	1903	67	Joe Morgan	CIN	1976	60
Jimmy Sheckard	BKN	1903	67	Gene Richards	SD	1980	60

Rickey Henderson *(opposite page)* studies the pitcher's motion as he takes his lead off first base. Henderson broke Ty Cobb's 65-year-old AL stolen base record by stealing 100 bases in 1980.

One of the most exciting developments in baseball in the past 15 years has been the rediscovery of the stolen base. The steal fell out of favor after the home-run explosion of the 1920s, when managers started waiting for the one big hit that would score a handful of runs at once.

More than any other base runner, Maury Wills brought back base stealing and made it part of today's game. Wills argued that there was no such thing as an unimportant stolen base, that it was worth it to steal at any time in any game. Before Wills, runners never stole when their team trailed by three or more runs, since you couldn't afford to lose a base runner, or when their team led by three or more runs, since you didn't want to embarrass your opponent.

Wills and Lou Brock showed just how disruptive the threat of a stolen base can be. With a great base-stealer on first base, the pitcher has to concentrate on keeping him from getting a big lead. The first baseman has to stay close to the base for a possible pick-off attempt, the catcher has to be ready to throw down to second, and the second baseman and shortstop have to be ready to take the catcher's throw. All of this distracts them from the business of getting the batter out.

Lou Brock gets his fast start off first base. The Cardinals' base-stealer relied on his knowledge of pitchers and his ability to take off quickly to pile up his career stolen base record.

BATTING RECORDS

Most Stolen Bases, Career

Player	SB
Lou Brock	938
Ty Cobb	892
Eddie Collins	743
Max Carey	738
Honus Wagner	703
Bert Campaneris	638
Joe Morgan	625
Maury Wills	586
Luis Aparicio	506
Clyde Milan	495
Cesar Cedeno	475
Jimmy Sheckard	460
Bobby Bonds	456
Sherry Magee	441
Tris Speaker	433
Bob Bescher	427
Frankie Frisch	419
Tommy Harper	408
Frank Chance	405
Donie Bush	403
Willie Davis	398
Dave Lopes	398
Ron LeFlore	391

Most Stolen Bases, Game, AL

Player	Team	Date	SB
Eddie Collins	PHI	Sep 11, 1912	6
	PHI	Sep 22, 1912	6
Clyde Milan	WAS	Jun 14, 1912	5
Johnny Neun	DET	Jul 9, 1927	5
Amos Otis	KC	Sep 7, 1971	5
Bert Campaneris	OAK	Apr 24, 1976	5

Most Stolen Bases, Game, NL

Player	Team	Date	SB
Dan McGann	NY	May 27, 1904	5
Dave Lopes	LA	Aug 24, 1974	5

The attempted steal of home has always been one of baseball's most electrifying plays. The runner dances off third, often dashing halfway home before returning to the base, trying to rattle the pitcher. Finally, the runner takes off for the plate as the pitcher starts his motion. If the pitcher hurries his throw to the plate, he may well throw the ball away.

Ty Cobb terrified American League pitchers for 24 years. A great hitter and base runner, he may have been the roughest player of all time. He is said to have filed the spikes on his shoes until they were razor sharp. Then he slid into a base with his spikes high, daring the fielders to tag him on the sharp metal. Cobb stole second, third, and home in one inning three times—once on three straight pitches!

The steal of home is no longer as much a part of the game as it was in Cobb's day. When it comes, it is usually as part of a delayed double steal. A runner breaks from first to second, and the runner on third waits for the catcher to throw to second before breaking for the plate. This kind of steal of home depends more on smart base-running than sheer speed. Oddly, in racking up a record 938 steals, Lou Brock *never* stole home.

Most Steals of Home, Career

Player	Total	Player	Total
Ty Cobb	35	Max Carey	14
George Burns	27	Fritz Maisel	14
Wildfire Schulte	22	Vic Saier	14
Johnny Evers	21	Honus Wagner	14
Jackie Robinson	19	Heinie Zimmerman	13
Frankie Frisch	19	Harry Hooper	11
George Sisler	19	Fred Merkle	11
Jimmy Sheckard	18	George Moriarty	11
Eddie Collins	17	Braggo Roth	11
Joe Tinker	17	Shano Collins	10
Larry Doyle	17	Buck Herzog	10
Rod Carew	16	Jimmy Johnston	10
Lou Gehrig	15	Babe Ruth	10
Tris Speaker	15	Bill Werber	10
Ben Chapman	14	Ross Youngs	10

BATTING RECORDS

Stole 2nd, 3rd, and Home in One Game, AL

Player	Team	Date
Dave Fultz	PHI	Sep 4, 1902
Wild Bill Donovan	DET	May 7, 1906
Bill Coughlin	DET	Jun 6, 1906
Ty Cobb	DET	Sep 2, 1907
	DET	Jul 23, 1909
	DET	Jul 12, 1911
	DET	Jul 4, 1912
Joe Jackson	CLE	Aug 11, 1912
Eddie Collins	PHI	Sep 22, 1912
Eddie Ainsmith	WAS	Jun 26, 1913
Red Faber	CHI	Jul 14, 1915
Danny Moeller	WAS	Jul 19, 1915
Fritz Maisel	NY	Aug 17, 1915
Ty Cobb	DET	Jun 18, 1917
Buck Weaver	CHI	Sep 6, 1919
Braggo Roth	WAS	May 31, 1920
Ty Cobb	DET	Aug 10, 1924
Bob Meusel	NY	May 16, 1927
Jackie Tavener	DET	Jul 10, 1927
	DET	Jul 25, 1928
Don Kolloway	CHI	Jun 28, 1941
Rod Carew	MIN	May 18, 1969
Dave Nelson	TEX	Aug 30, 1974

Stole 2nd, 3rd, and Home in One Game, NL

Player	Team	Date
Honus Wagner	PIT	Jun 15, 1902
	PIT	Sep 25, 1907
Buck Herzog	NY	Sep 9, 1908
Hans Lobert	CIN	Sep 27, 1908
Honus Wagner	PIT	May 2, 1909
Bill O'Hara	NY	Aug 8, 1909
Dode Paskert	CIN	May 23, 1910
Wilbur Good	CHI	Aug 18, 1915
Jimmy Johnston	BKN	Sep 22, 1916
Greasy Neale	CIN	Aug 15, 1919
Max Carey	PIT	Aug 18, 1923
	PIT	Aug 26, 1925
Harvey Hendrick	BKN	Jun 12, 1928
Jackie Robinson	BKN	Apr 23, 1954
Pete Rose	PHI	May 11, 1980

In 1941, Joe DiMaggio of the New York Yankees hit safely in 56 consecutive games to set one of baseball's greatest records. No one has even come close to breaking it. The streak started on May 15, and it wasn't stopped until two months later, on July 17. Along the way, DiMaggio shattered the previous Yankee club record of 29, shared by Roger Peckinpaugh (1919) and Earle Combs (1931), the American League mark of 41, set by George Sisler of the St. Louis Browns in 1922, and Wee Willie Keeler's all-time major league record of 44, set with the old Baltimore Orioles of the National League in 1897. The day after the streak was stopped by the combined pitching of Al Smith and Jim Bagby of the Indians, DiMaggio began another streak that lasted 16 games. This gave him a hit in 72 out of 73 games, putting him past Bill Dahlen of the Chicago Cubs, who had hit safely in 70 of 71 games back in 1894.

The most serious challenge to DiMaggio's record came in 1978, when Pete Rose hit in 44 consecutive games, tying Keeler's National League record. Rose was stopped by Atlanta's Larry McWilliams and Gene Garber on July 31, 12 games short of DiMaggio's incredible mark.

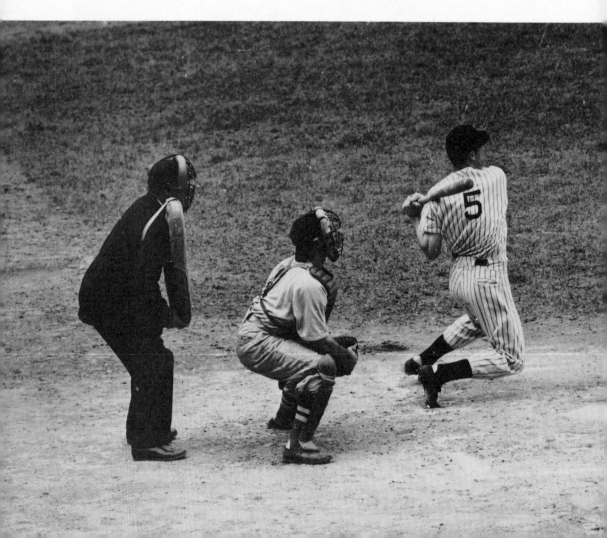

Longest Hitting Streaks, AL

Player	Team		G	Player	Team		G
Joe DiMaggio	NY	1941	56	Socks Seybold	PHI	1901	27
George Sisler	STL	1922	41	Hal Chase	NY	1907	27
Ty Cobb	DET	1911	40	Sam Rice	WAS	1925	27
	DET	1917	35	John Stone	DET	1930	27
George Sisler	STL	1925	34	Heinie Manush	WAS	1930	27
John Stone	DET	1930	34	Al Simmons	PHI	1931	27
George McQuinn	STL	1938	34	Luke Appling	CHI	1936	27
Dom DiMaggio	BOS	1949	34	Gee Walker	DET	1936	27
Heinie Manush	WAS	1934	33	Bruce Campbell	DET	1941	27
Sam Rice	WAS	1924	31	Bob Dillinger	STL	1948	27
Ken Landreaux	MIN	1980	31	Dom DiMaggio	BOS	1951	27
Tris Speaker	BOS	1912	30	Dale Mitchell	CLE	1953	27
Goose Goslin	DET	1934	30	Ron LeFlore	DET	1978	27
Ron LeFlore	DET	1976	30	Buck Freeman	BOS	1902	26
George Brett	KC	1980	30	Harry Bay	CLE	1902	26
Bill Bradley	CLE	1902	29	Hobe Ferris	STL	1908	26
Roger Peckinpaugh	NY	1919	29	Babe Ruth	NY	1921	26
Bill Lamar	PHI	1925	29	Heinie Manush	WAS	1933	26
Dale Alexander	DET	1930	29	Bob Johnson	PHI	1934	26
Earle Combs	NY	1931	29	Guy Curtright	CHI	1943	26
Pete Fox	DET	1935	29	Johnny Pesky	BOS	1947	26
Mel Almada	STL	1938	29	Ty Cobb	DET	1906	25
Joe Gordon	NY	1942	29	Bucky Harris	WAS	1925	25
Nap Lajoie	PHI	1901	28	Goose Goslin	WAS	1928	25
Joe Jackson	CLE	1911	28	Catfish Metkovich	BOS	1944	25
Ken Williams	STL	1922	28	Jimmie Foxx	PHI	1929	24
Bing Miller	PHI	1929	28	Cecil Travis	WAS	1941	24
Sam Rice	WAS	1930	28	Chico Carrasquel	CHI	1950	24
Heinie Manush	WAS	1932	28	Ferris Fain	PHI	1952	24
Doc Cramer	PHI	1932	28	Lenny Green	MIN	1961	24
Hal Trosky	CLE	1936	28	Dave May	MIL	1973	24
				Mickey Rivers	TEX	1980	24

Joe DiMaggio's phenomenal 56-game hitting streak was the high point of a career noted for consistent excellence *(opposite page).* His Yankee teammates claim they never saw him make a mental mistake on a baseball diamond.

BATTING RECORDS

Longest Hitting Streaks, NL

Player	Team		G	Player	Team		G
Willie Keeler	BAL	1897	44	Vada Pinson	CIN	1965	27
Pete Rose	CIN	1978	44	Glenn Beckert	CHI	1968	27
Bill Dahlen	CHI	1894	42	Willie Keeler	BAL	1896	26
Tommy Holmes	BOS	1945	37	George Decker	CHI	1896	26
Billy Hamilton	BOS	1896	36	Bill Sweeney	BOS	1911	26
Fred Clarke	LOU	1895	35	Zack Wheat	BKN	1918	26
George Davis	NY	1893	33	Goldie Rapp	PHI	1921	26
Rogers Hornsby	STL	1922	33	Pie Traynor	PIT	1923	26
Ed Delahanty	PHI	1899	31	Chuck Klein	PHI	1930	26
Willie Davis	LA	1969	31		PHI	1930	26
Rico Carty	ATL	1970	31	Gabby Hartnett	CHI	1937	26
Elmer Smith	CIN	1898	30	Danny O'Connell	PIT	1953	26
Stan Musial	STL	1950	30	Lou Brock	STL	1971	26
Zack Wheat	BKN	1916	29	Glenn Beckert	CHI	1973	26
Harry Walker	STL	1943	29	Jack Clark	SF	1978	26
Ken Boyer	STL	1959	29	Clyde Barnhart	PIT	1925	25
Rowland Office	ATL	1976	29	Rube Bressler	CIN	1927	25
Lloyd Waner	PIT	1932	28	Hughie Critz	CIN	1927	25
Joe Medwick	STL	1935	28	Harvey Hendrick	BKN	1929	25
Red Schoendienst	STL	1954	28	Charlie Grimm	CHI	1933	25
Ron Santo	CHI	1966	28	Fred Lindstrom	PIT	1933	25
Piano Legs Hickman	NY	1900	27	Buzz Boyle	BKN	1934	25
Edd Roush	CIN	1920	27	Hank Aaron	MIL	1956	25
	CIN	1924	27		MIL	1962	25
Hack Wilson	CHI	1929	27	Pete Rose	CIN	1967	25
Joe Medwick	BKN	1942	27	Willie Davis	LA	1971	25
Duke Snider	BKN	1953	27				

Willie Keeler of the old Baltimore Orioles *(left),* described his batting style very simply: "Hit 'em where they ain't." He choked way up on the bat and punched the ball just over the infielders' heads in putting together his 44-game hitting streak. This NL record was matched by **Pete Rose** *(below),* here hitting safely in his 44th straight game in 1978. Rose revived the forgotten art of hitting singles, showing that a batter doesn't have to hit home runs to help his team.

Lou Gehrig, "The Iron Horse."

On June 1, 1925, New York Yankee first baseman Wally Pipp missed a game with a bad headache. He was replaced by rookie Lou Gehrig. For the next 14 years, Gehrig appeared in the Yankee line-up every single day, for an awesome total of 2,130 straight games. Of all of baseball's great records, this one seems most likely to last forever.

The biggest threat to Gehrig's streak came on July 13, 1934. The Yankees were playing in Detroit, and Gehrig had such a severe case of lumbago that he had to be helped off the field in the first inning. It looked as if his streak would end at 1,426 games. But the next day, Gehrig was listed in the Yankee line-up at shortstop, as the lead-off hitter. He was barely able to stand up, but he banged out a lead-off single and was taken out for a pinch runner, his streak intact. Still wobbly, Gehrig returned to the line-up at first base the next day and collected four hits, three of them doubles, in four times at bat.

Gehrig's streak ended tragically. On May 2, 1939, suffering from amyotrophic lateral sclerosis, a rare disease affecting the nerves and muscles, Gehrig pulled himself from the line-up.

Just how incredible is Gehrig's record? The closest active player is Steve Garvey of the Los Angeles Dodgers, who hasn't missed a game since 1975. To overtake Gehrig, Garvey must play in every game through the 1988 season, at which time he'll be thirty-nine years old.

Most Consecutive Games Played

Player	G
Lou Gehrig	2130
Everett Scott	1307
Billy Williams	1117
Joe Sewell	1103
Stan Musial	895
Steve Garvey	836
Eddie Yost	829
Gus Suhr	822
Nellie Fox	798
Richie Ashburn	730
Ernie Banks	717
Pete Rose	678
Earl Averill	673
Frank McCormick	652
Sandy Alomar	648
Eddie Brown	618
Roy McMillan	585
George Pinckney	577
Steve Brodie	574
Aaron Ward	565
Candy LaChance	540
Buck Freeman	535
Fred Luderus	533
Clyde Milan	511
Charlie Gehringer	511
Vada Pinson	508
Charlie Gehringer	504

BATTING RECORDS

Most Consecutive Hits, AL

Player	Team		H
Pinky Higgins	BOS	1938	12
Walt Dropo	BOS	1952	12
Tris Speaker	CLE	1920	11
Johnny Pesky	BOS	1946	11
George Sisler	STL	1921	10
Harry Heilmann	DET	1922	10
Harry McCurdy	CHI	1926	10
Doc Johnston	CLE	1919	9
Ty Cobb	DET	1925	9
Hal Trosky	CLE	1936	9

Most Consecutive Hits, NL

Player	Team		H
Ed Delahanty	PHI	1897	10
Jake Gettman	WAS	1897	10
Ed Konetchy	BKN	1919	10
Kiki Cuyler	PIT	1925	10
Chick Hafey	STL	1929	10
Joe Medwick	STL	1936	10
Buddy Hassett	BOS	1940	10
Woody Williams	CIN	1943	10
Joe Kelley	BAL	1894	9
Rogers Hornsby	STL	1924	9
Taylor Douthit	STL	1926	9
Babe Herman	BKN	1926	9
Bill Jurges	NY	1941	9
Terry Moore	STL	1947	9
Dave Philley	PHI	1958	
	PHI	1959	9
Ron Cey	LA	1977	9

The Hitters Take Charge: 1920-1939

Babe Ruth's 29 homers in 1919, startling as they were, scarcely prepared fans for what was to come. He exploded for 54 in 1920, 35 more than his nearest competitor. The home run brought glamour to Ruth and to the game itself. Fans flocked to the ball parks to see this exciting new weapon and this great new star. The team owners saw that Ruth's blasts took the public's mind off the Black Sox scandal, so they livened up the ball to make it go farther. This new "rabbit ball," so named for the way it "jumped" off the bat, produced more home runs, more excitement, and greater and greater attendance. In 1920, Ruth was the only hitter in baseball with 20 or more homers; by 1930, almost every team had one top home-run hitter, and many clubs had two or three.

Because of the new ball, many of the game's most enduring hitting records were set in these years: George Sisler of the St. Louis Browns had 257 hits in 1920; Ruth broke his own home-run mark with 59 in 1921 and again with 60 in 1927; Rogers Hornsby batted .424 for the Cardinals in 1924. The crest of this hitting wave came in 1930, when Bill Terry became the last National Leaguer to top .400, Hack Wilson drove in 190 runs for the Cubs, and the batting average for the National League as a whole was .303.

The Yankees played in 11 of the 20 World Series between 1920 and 1939, winning 8 of them. With future Hall of Famers Ruth, Lou Gehrig, Earle Combs, Waite Hoyt, and Herb Pennock in the 1920s and Gehrig, Joe DiMaggio, Bill Dickey, Lefty Gomez, and Red Ruffing in the 1930s, the Yankees established themselves as the team to beat every year.

The glory of those Yankee teams makes it easy to overlook the other great teams of the 1920s and 1930s. The Philadelphia Athletics, who beat out the Yankees for AL titles in 1929, 1930, and 1931, had four future Hall of Famers of their own in Jimmie Foxx, Mickey Cochrane, Al Simmons, and Lefty Grove. The Athletics gave the Cubs a graphic display of their fire power in the fourth game of the 1929 World Series when, trailing 8-0, they exploded for ten runs in the seventh inning and went on to win the Series four games to one. Another legendary team was the St. Louis Cardinals' "Gas House Gang" of 1934, which defeated the Detroit Tigers in a memorable seven-game Series. Before the Series began, Cardinal pitcher Dizzy Dean predicted, "Me and Paul will win 'em all." Sure enough, Dizzy won two games and his brother Paul won two others against a high-powered Tigers team that boasted seven .300 hitters.

THE GAS HOUSE GANG

Of all the wild and rowdy baseball clubs, few matched the rambunctious St. Louis Cardinals of 1934. The pitching staff was led by the Dean brothers *(top)*, Paul *(left)* and Dizzy *(right)*. Paul was as quiet as Dizzy was noisy. Diz' used to boast loudly of the great feats he would perform and then make good on his predictions. "If you can do it, it ain't braggin'," he explained. The regular line-up included second baseman-manager Frankie Frisch, "The Fordham Flash"; third baseman Pepper Martin, "The Wild Horse of the Osage"; and leftfielder Joe "Ducky" Medwick *(bottom, left to right)*.

THE GOLDEN AGE

The Roaring Twenties has been called the Golden Age of Sports. The great stars of the period included football player Harold "Red" Grange, heavyweight boxing champion Jack Dempsey, swimming sensation Johnny Weismuller (who went on to movie fame as Tarzan), and golfer Bobby Jones. But the most glamorous of all these stars, as reflected in the happy faces swarming around him, was the Sultan of Swat, Babe Ruth. Ruth's exploits made baseball America's favorite sport.

THE BABE

He broke in as a left-handed pitcher for the Boston Red Sox *(left),* and many think he was one of the best, with an ERA of 2.28 in five years on the mound. But he was too good a hitter to appear in the line-up only once every four days, so he became an outfielder between pitching starts. The day the Red Sox sold him to New York marked a turning point in baseball history: Since then, the Yankees have won 22 World Series, and the Red Sox have won none. He hit one home run every twelve times at bat, by far the best average in history, and drew more walks from understandably nervous pitchers than any other player. Babe Ruth was the most powerful slugger, the most exciting player, and the greatest star the game has ever known.

LOU GEHRIG

It was Lou Gehrig's misfortune to spend his career in the shadow of Babe Ruth. Gehrig's shy, unassuming manner made him easy to overlook next to Ruth's outgoing ways. But together they made up the heart of some of the most powerful teams in baseball history—the great Yankee clubs of the 1920s and 1930s. Gehrig's batting record shows him to be nearly the equal of Ruth; he was the first American Leaguer to hit four home runs in one game, and his total of 184 RBIs in 1931 is the highest in AL history. His career was cut short by a tragic illness, and he was forced to retire in 1939 at age 36. On July 4, 1939, Lou Gehrig Day at Yankee Stadium *(below),* he stood before the cheering fans and said, "I'm the luckiest man in the world." He died just two years later.

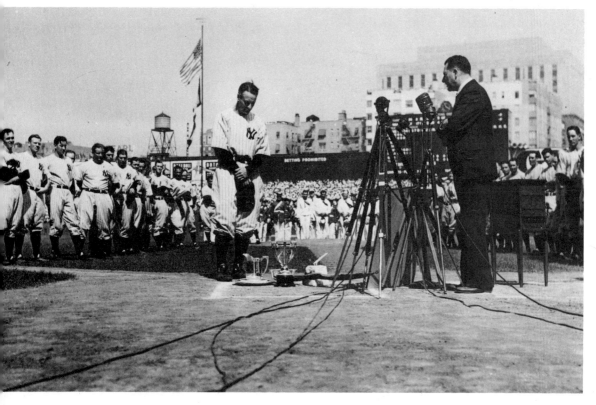

HORNSBY AND WILSON

Hack Wilson *(left)* and Rogers Hornsby *(right)* set many of the most enduring NL records during the 1920s and early 1930s. Wilson capped his slugging career with his spectacular 1930 season, when he hit 56 home runs and drove in 190 runs; both are NL records. Hornsby, known as "The Rajah," combined slugging power with the ability to hit for a high batting average. While playing for the Cardinals in the early 1920s, Hornsby won six straight batting titles. His .424 average in 1924 is the highest in the majors since 1900, and he is the only National Leaguer to win two Triple Crowns, in 1922 and 1925.

Pitching
Records

The undisputed king of shutouts has to be Walter Johnson, who spent his entire big league career with the Washington Senators.

Johnson holds the major league record for most career shutouts. He shut out one club, the Philadelphia Athletics, a total of twenty-three times—another record. Seven of his shutouts came on Opening Day—still another record. Once he even pitched three shutouts in four days, all against the Yankees.

Johnson won the most 1–0 games, 38, and lost the most 1–0 games, 28. He also had the most shutouts pitched against him, 65.

To sum it all up, Johnson pitched in 178 decisions that resulted in shutouts and 66 that ended 1–0.

Most Shutouts, Career

Player	ShO	Player	ShO
Walter Johnson	113	Babe Adams	46
Grover Alexander	90	Bob Feller	46
Christy Mathewson	83	Doc White	46
Cy Young	77	Whitey Ford	45
Eddie Plank	69	Addie Joss	45
Warren Spahn	63	Robin Roberts	45
Ed Walsh	58	Steve Carlton	45
Three Finger Brown	58	Nolan Ryan	44
Pud Galvin	56	Milt Pappas	43
Bob Gibson	56	Tommy John	42
Tom Seaver	53	Catfish Hunter	42
Don Sutton	52	Bucky Walters	42
Gaylord Perry	52	Bert Blyleven	41
Juan Marichal	51	Chief Bender	41
Jim Palmer	51	Mickey Lolich	41
Rube Waddell	50	Hippo Vaughn	40
Vic Willis	50	Mickey Welch	40
Luis Tiant	49	Larry French	40
Early Wynn	49	Tim Keefe	40
Don Drysdale	49	Claude Osteen	40
Kid Nichols	48	Mel Stottlemyre	40
Ferguson Jenkins	47	Jim Bunning	40
Jack Powell	47	Sandy Koufax	40
Red Ruffing	46		

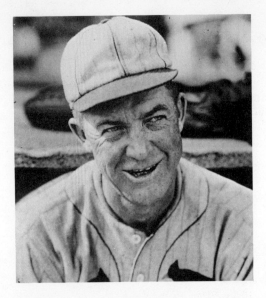

Grover Cleveland Alexander, "Old Pete," won 33 games for the 1916 Phillies, including a record 16 shutouts.

Most Shutouts, Season, AL

Player	Team		ShO	Player	Team		ShO
Jack Coombs	PHI	1910	13	Addie Joss	CLE	1906	9
Ed Walsh	CHI	1908	12		CLE	1908	9
Walter Johnson	WAS	1913	12	Babe Ruth	BOS	1916	9
Dean Chance	LA	1964	11	Stan Coveleski	CLE	1917	9
Cy Young	BOS	1904	10	Bob Porterfield	WAS	1953	9
Ed Walsh	CHI	1906	10	Luis Tiant	CLE	1968	9
Joe Wood	BOS	1912	10	Denny McLain	DET	1969	9
Walter Johnson	WAS	1914	10	Nolan Ryan	CAL	1972	9
Bob Feller	CLE	1946	10	Bert Blyleven	MIN	1973	9
Bob Lemon	CLE	1948	10	Ron Guidry	NY	1978	9
Jim Palmer	BAL	1975	10				

Most Shutouts, Season, NL

Player	Team		ShO	Player	Team		ShO
George Bradley	STL	1876	16	Tommy Bond	BOS	1878	9
Grover Alexander	PHI	1916	16	Monte Ward	PRO	1880	9
Bob Gibson	STL	1968	13	George Derby	DET	1881	9
Tommy Bond	BOS	1879	12	Cy Young	CLE	1892	9
Pud Galvin	BUF	1884	12	Al Spalding	CHI	1876	9
Christy Mathewson	NY	1908	12	Christy Mathewson	NY	1907	9
Grover Alexander	PHI	1915	12	Orval Overall	CHI	1907	9
Old Hoss Radbourn	PRO	1885	11	Three Finger Brown	CHI	1908	9
Sandy Koufax	LA	1963	11	Joe McGinnity	NY	1904	9
John Clarkson	CHI	1885	10	Orval Overall	CHI	1909	9
Carl Hubbell	NY	1933	10	Grover Alexander	PHI	1913	9
Three Finger Brown	CHI	1906	10		CHI	1919	9
Juan Marichal	SF	1965	10	Bill Lee	CHI	1938	9
Mort Cooper	STL	1942	10	Christy Mathewson	NY	1905	9

PITCHING RECORDS

Shutout with Most Hits Allowed, AL

Player	Team	Date	Score	H	Opp.
Milt Gaston	WAS	Jul 10, 1928	9-0	14	CLE
Duster Mails	CLE	Jul 10, 1921	10-0	12	PHI
Milt Gaston	STL	Sep 12, 1926	1-0	12	BOS
Garland Buckeye	CLE	Sep 16, 1926	5-0	12	NY
Stan Bahnsen	CHI	Jun 21, 1973	2-0	12	OAK
Harry Howell	STL	Jun 23, 1906	4-0	11	CLE
Jack Chesbro	NY	Aug 19, 1908	8-0	11	DET
Waite Hoyt	NY	Jul 1, 1924	7-0	11	PHI
Earl Whitehill	DET	Jul 5, 1924	3-0	11	CHI
Herb Pennock	NY	Jun 3, 1933	4-0	11	BOS
Robin Roberts	BAL	Jul 17, 1964	5-0	11	DET
Jim Kaat	MIN	Apr 11, 1971	6-0	11	CHI
Marty Pattin	MIL	Jun 26, 1971	5-0	11	MIN
Gaylord Perry	TEX	Jul 28, 1977	3-0	11	TOR

Shutout with Most Hits Allowed, NL

Player	Team	Date	Score	H	Opp.
Larry Cheney	CHI	Sep 14, 1913	7-0	14	NY
Scott Stratton	LOU	Sep 19, 1893	3-0	13	NY
Ned Garvin	CHI	Sep 22, 1899	3-0	13	BOS
Bill Lee	CHI	Sep 17, 1938	4-0	13	NY
Nixey Callahan	CHI	Apr 30, 1899	4-0	12	STL
Pol Perritt	NY	Sep 14, 1917	5-0	12	BOS
Rube Benton	NY	Aug 28, 1920	4-0	12	CIN
Leon Cadore	BKN	Sep 4, 1920	10-0	12	BOS
George Smith	PHI	Aug 12, 1921	4-0	12	BOS
Hal Schumacher	NY	Jul 19, 1934	4-0	12	CIN
Fritz Ostermueller	PIT	May 17, 1947	4-0	12	CIN
Bob Friend	PIT	Sep 24, 1959	6-0	12	STL
Jack Taylor	PHI	May 31, 1897	14-0	11	LOU
Jouett Meekin	NY	Jun 17, 1897	5-0	11	CLE
Bill Damman	CIN	May 6, 1899	1-0	11	STL
Charlie Case	PIT	Aug 1, 1904	4-0	11	CHI
Al Mattern	BOS	Jul 22, 1908	4-0	11	STL
Babe Adams	PIT	Aug 9, 1910	14-0	11	BOS
Three Finger Brown	CHI	Aug 15, 1910	14-0	11	BKN
Christy Mathewson	NY	Aug 11, 1911	6-0	11	PHI
Dan Griner	STL	Jun 14, 1913	1-0	11	CHI
Scott Perry	CHI	Sep 14, 1916	2-0	11	BOS
Fred Baczewski	CIN	Aug 10, 1954	6-0	11	PIT
Bob Purkey	CIN	Aug 15, 1960	4-0	11	MIL
Billy O'Dell	SF	Sep 30, 1963	5-0	11	PHI

Batters dream of hitting the game-winning home run. Fielders dream of making diving catches to save a close game. Pitchers dream of pitching no-hitters.

In all the world of sports, there's nothing that can compare to the sustained tension of the last innings of a no-hitter, especially when the pitcher is pitching before his home crowd. The crowd reacts to every pitch, roaring for every strike, booing at every called ball, holding its breath when the ball is hit and not releasing it until the batter is out. Superstitious fans and broadcasters won't even utter the dreaded word *no-hitter* for fear of jinxing the pitcher. (For some reason, the words *perfect game* can be spoken safely, but *no-hitter* must never be mentioned.)

Some more no-hit lore: Johnny Vandermeer is the only pitcher to pitch two consecutive no-hitters. Ewell Blackwell came close, but gave up a hit in the ninth inning of his second game. Bobo Holloman pitched a no-hitter in his first major league start. It was the only complete game of his career. Bob Feller pitched the only Opening Day no-hitter, in 1940. And Fred Toney and Jim "Hippo" Vaughn pitched the only nine-inning double no-hitter on May 2, 1917. Vaughn gave up the first hit of the game in the tenth inning and lost 1–0.

No-Hitters, AL

Player	Team	Date	Score	BB	SO	E	Opp.	Opp. Pitcher
Earl Moore	CLE	May 9, 1901	2-4	4	4	1	CHI	John Katoll
Nixey Callahan	CHI	Sep 20, 1902	3-0	2	2	1	DET	Wish Egan
Cy Young	BOS	May 5, 1904	3-0	0	8	0	PHI	Rube Waddell
Jesse Tannehill	BOS	Aug 17, 1904	6-0	1	4	0	CHI	Ed Walsh
Weldon Henley	PHI	Jul 22, 1905	6-0	3	5	1	STL	Barney Pelty
Frank Smith	CHI	Sep 6, 1905	15-0	3	8	0	DET	Jimmy Wiggs
Bill Dinneen	BOS	Sep 27, 1905	2-0	2	6	0	CHI	Frank Owen
Cy Young	BOS	Jun 30, 1908	8-0	1	2	0	NY	Rube Manning
Bob Rhoads	CLE	Sep 18, 1908	2-1	2	2	2	BOS	Frank Arellanes
Frank Smith	CHI	Sep 20, 1908	1-0	1	2	1	PHI	Eddie Plank
Addie Joss	CLE	Oct 2, 1908	1-0	0	3	0	CHI	Ed Walsh
	CLE	Apr 20, 1910	1-0	2	2	1	CHI	Doc White
Chief Bender	PHI	May 12, 1910	4-0	1	4	0	CLE	Fred Linke
Tom Hughes	NY	Aug 30, 1910	0-5	0	4	1	CLE	George Kahler
Joe Wood	BOS	Jul 29, 1911	5-0	2	12	1	STL	Joe Lake
Ed Walsh	CHI	Aug 27, 1911	5-0	1	8	0	BOS	Ray Collins
George Mullin	DET	Jul 4, 1912	7-0	5	5	1	STL	Willie Adams
Earl Hamilton	STL	Aug 30, 1912	5-1	2	3	2	DET	Jean Dubuc
Jim Scott	CHI	May 14, 1914	0-1	3	2	3	WAS	Doc Ayers
Joe Benz	CHI	May 31, 1914	6-1	2	6	3	CLE	Abe Bowman
Rube Foster	BOS	Jun 21, 1916	2-0	3	3	0	NY	Bob Shawkey
Joe Bush	PHI	Aug 26, 1916	5-0	1	7	0	CLE	Stan Coveleski
Dutch Leonard	BOS	Aug 30, 1916	4-0	2	5	0	STL	Carl Weilman
Eddie Cicotte	CHI	Apr 14, 1917	11-0	3	5	1	STL	Earl Hamilton
George Mogridge	NY	Apr 24, 1917	2-1	3	3	3	BOS	Dutch Leonard
Ernie Koob	STL	May 5, 1917	1-0	5	2	2	CHI	Eddie Cicotte
Bob Groom	STL	May 6, 1917	3-0	3	4	0	CHI	Joe Benz
Ernie Shore	BOS	Jun 23, 1917	4-0	0	2	0	WAS	Doc Ayers
Dutch Leonard	BOS	Jun 3, 1918	5-0	1	4	0	DET	Hooks Dauss
Ray Caldwell	CLE	Sep 10, 1919	3-0	1	5	1	NY	Carl Mays
Walter Johnson	WAS	Jul 1, 1920	1-0	0	10	1	BOS	Harry Harper
Charlie Robertson	CHI	Apr 30, 1922	2-0	0	6	0	DET	Herman Pillette

No-Hitters, AL (continued)

Player	Team	Date	Score	BB	SO	E	Opp.	Opp. Pitcher
Sad Sam Jones	NY	Sep 4, 1923	2-0	1	0	1	PHI	Bob Hasty
Howard Ehmke	BOS	Sep 7, 1923	4-0	1	1	1	PHI	Slim Harriss
Ted Lyons	CHI	Aug 21, 1926	6-0	1	2	1	BOS	
Wes Ferrell	CLE	Apr 29, 1931	9-0	3	8	3	STL	Sam Gray
Bobby Burke	WAS	Aug 8, 1931	5-0	5	8	0	BOS	Wilcy Moore
Bobo Newsom	STL	Sep 18, 1934	1-2	7	9	3	BOS	Wes Ferrell
Vern Kennedy	CHI	Aug 31, 1935	5-0	4	5	0	CLE	Willis Hudlin
Bill Dietrich	CHI	Jun 1, 1937	8-0	2	5	1	STL	Chief Hogsett
Monte Pearson	NY	Aug 27, 1938	13-0	2	7	0	CLE	John Humphries
Bob Feller	CLE	Apr 16, 1940	1-0	5	8	1	CHI	Eddie Smith
Dick Fowler	PHI	Sep 9, 1945	1-0	4	6	0	STL	Ox Miller
Bob Feller	CLE	Apr 30, 1946	1-0	5	11	2	NY	Bill Bevens
Don Black	CLE	Jul 10, 1947	3-0	6	5	0	PHI	Bill McCahan
Bill McCahan	PHI	Sep 3, 1947	3-0	0	2	1	WAS	Ray Scarborough
Bob Lemon	CLE	Jun 30, 1948	2-0	3	4	0	DET	Art Houtteman
Bob Feller	CLE	Jul 1, 1951	2-1	3	5	2	DET	Bob Cain
Allie Reynolds	NY	Jul 12, 1951	1-0	3	4	1	CLE	Bob Feller
	NY	Sep 28, 1951	8-0	4	9	1	BOS	Mel Parnell
Virgil Trucks	DET	May 15, 1952	1-0	1	7	3	WAS	Bob Porterfield
	DET	Aug 25, 1952	1-0	1	8	2	NY	Bill Miller
Bobo Holloman	STL	May 6, 1953	6-0	5	3	1	PHI	Morrie Martin
Mel Parnell	BOS	Jul 14, 1956	4-0	2	4	0	CHI	Jim McDonald
Don Larsen	NY	Oct 8, 1956	2-0	0	7	0	BKN	Sal Maglie
Bob Keegan	CHI	Aug 20, 1957	6-0	2	1	0	WAS	Chuck Stobbs
Jim Bunning	DET	Jul 20, 1958	3-0	2	12	0	BOS	Frank Sullivan
Hoyt Wilhelm	BAL	Sep 20, 1958	1-0	2	8	0	NY	Don Larsen
Bo Belinsky	LA	May 1, 1962	2-0	5	9	1	BAL	Steve Barber
Earl Wilson	BOS	Jun 26, 1962	2-0	4	5	0	LA	Bo Belinsky
Bill Monbouquette	BOS	Aug 1, 1962	1-0	1	7	0	CHI	Early Wynn
Jack Kralick	MIN	Aug 26, 1962	1-0	1	3	0	KC	Bill Fischer
Dave Morehead	BOS	Sep 16, 1965	2-0	1	8	0	CLE	Luis Tiant
Sonny Siebert	CLE	Jun 10, 1966	2-0	1	7	1	WAS	Phil Ortega
Dean Chance	MIN	Aug 25, 1967	2-1	5	9	1	CLE	Sonny Siebert
Joe Horlen	CHI	Sep 10, 1967	6-0	0	4	1	DET	Joe Sparma
Tom Phoebus	BAL	Apr 27, 1968	6-0	3	9	0	BOS	Gary Waslewski
Catfish Hunter	OAK	May 8, 1968	4-0	0	11	0	MIN	Dave Boswell
Jim Palmer	BAL	Aug 13, 1969	8-0	6	8	2	OAK	Chuck Dobson
Clyde Wright	CAL	Jul 3, 1970	4-0	3	1	0	OAK	
Vida Blue	OAK	Sep 21, 1970	6-0	1	9	0	MIN	Jim Perry
Steve Busby	KC	Apr 27, 1973	3-0	6	4	0	DET	
Nolan Ryan	CAL	May 15, 1973	3-0	3	12	0	KC	Bruce Dal Canton
	CAL	Jul 15, 1973	6-0	4	17	0	DET	Jim Perry
Jim Bibby	TEX	Jul 30, 1973	8-0	6	13	0	OAK	Vida Blue
Steve Busby	KC	Jun 19, 1974	2-0	1	3	0	MIL	Clyde Wright
Dick Bosman	CLE	Jul 19, 1974	4-0	0	4	1	OAK	Dave Hamilton
Nolan Ryan	CAL	Sep 28, 1974	4-0	8	15	0	MIN	Joe Decker
	CAL	Jun 1, 1975	1-0	4	9	1	BAL	Ross Grimsley
Jim Colborn	KC	May 14, 1977	6-0	1	6	0	TEX	Tom Boggs
Dennis Eckersley	CLE	May 30, 1977	1-0	1	12	0	CAL	Frank Tanana
Bert Blyleven	TEX	Sep 22, 1977	6-0	1	7	0	CAL	Paul Hartzell

NO-HIT CATCHERS

The pitcher who hurls a no-hitter is immediately written into the record books and wins a place in baseball history. But what about the man behind the plate who called the pitches that silenced the opponents' bats?

The man who has caught the most no-hitters is **Ray Schalk** of the White Sox *(right)*. Schalk caught four no-hitters, one a perfect game, in his 17-year career. Eight catchers have caught three no-hitters: Yogi Berra, Roy Campanella, Bill Carrigan, Del Crandall, Johnny Edwards, Jim Hegan, Val Picinich, and Luke Sewell. Only two men, Gus Triandos and Jeff Torborg, have caught no-hitters in both leagues.

No-Hitters, NL

Player	Team	Date	Score	BB	SO	E	Opp.	Opp. Pitcher
George Bradley	STL	Jul 15, 1876	2-0	1	3	3	HAR	Tommy Bond
Lee Richmond	WOR	Jun 12, 1880	1-0	0	7	0	CLE	Jim McCormick
Monte Ward	PRO	Jun 17, 1880	5-0	0	7	0	BUF	Pud Galvin
Larry Corcoran	CHI	Aug 19, 1880	6-0	2	4	2	BOS	Tommy Bond
Pud Galvin	BUF	Aug 20, 1880	1-0	0	2	6	WOR	Fred Corey
Larry Corcoran	CHI	Sep 20, 1882	5-0	1	3	4	WOR	Frank Mountain
Old Hoss Radbourn	PRO	Jul 25, 1883	8-0	0	6	1	CLE	One Arm Daily
One Arm Daily	CLE	Sep 13, 1883	1-0	3	2	2	PHI	John Coleman
Larry Corcoran	CHI	Jun 27, 1884	6-0	1	6	6	PRO	Charlie Sweeney
Pud Galvin	BUF	Aug 4, 1884	18-0	0	7	2	DET	Frank Meinke
Charlie Buffinton	BOS	Aug 9, 1884	1-2	0	4	2	PRO	Old Hoss Radbourn
John Clarkson	CHI	Jul 27, 1885	4-0	0	4	5	PRO	
Charlie Ferguson	PHI	Aug 29, 1885	1-0	2	8	6	PRO	Dupee Shaw
Tom Lovett	BKN	Jun 22, 1891	4-0	3	4	0	NY	Amos Rusie
Amos Rusie	NY	Jul 31, 1891	6-0	8	4	2	BKN	Adonis Terry
Jack Stivetts	BOS	Aug 6, 1892	11-0	5	6	3	BKN	Ed Stein

No-Hitters, NL (continued)

Player	Team	Date	Score	BB	SO	E	Opp.	Opp. Pitcher
Ben Sanders	LOU	Aug 22, 1892	6-2	3	0	4	BAL	Sadie McMahon
Bumpus Jones	CIN	Oct 15, 1892	7-1	3	1	0	PIT	Mark Baldwin
Bill Hawke	BAL	Aug 16, 1893	5-0	2	6	0	WAS	George Stephens
Cy Young	CLE	Sep 18, 1897	6-0	1	3	3	CIN	Billy Rhines
Ted Breitenstein	CIN	Apr 22, 1898	11-0	1	2	1	PIT	Charlie Hastings
Jim Hughes	BAL	Apr 22, 1898	8-0	2	3	0	BOS	Ted Lewis
Red Donahue	PHI	Jul 8, 1898	5-0	2	1	0	BOS	Vic Willis
Walter Thornton	CHI	Aug 21, 1898	2-0	3	3	0	BKN	Brickyard Kennedy
Deacon Phillippe	LOU	May 25, 1899	7-0	2	1	0	NY	Ed Doheny
Vic Willis	BOS	Aug 7, 1899	7-1	4	5	3	WAS	Bill Dinneen
Noodles Hahn	CIN	Jul 12, 1900	4-0	2	8	1	PHI	Bill Bernhard
Christy Mathewson	NY	Jul 15, 1901	5-0	4	4	1	STL	Willie Sudhoff
Chick Fraser	PHI	Sep 18, 1903	10-0	5	4	4	CHI	Peaches Graham
Bob Wicker	CHI	Jun 11, 1904	1-0	1	10	1	NY	Joe McGinnity
Christy Mathewson	NY	Jun 13, 1905	1-0	0	2	2	CHI	Three Finger Brown
Johnny Lush	PHI	May 1, 1906	1-0	3	11	1	BKN	Mal Eason
Mal Eason	BKN	Jul 20, 1906	2-0	3	5	1	STL	Gus Thompson
Harry McIntire	BKN	Aug 1, 1906	0-1	1	8	1	PIT	Lefty Leifield
Big Jeff Pfeffer	BOS	May 8, 1907	6-0	1	3	1	CIN	Del Mason
Nick Maddox	PIT	Sep 20, 1907	2-1	3	5	2	BKN	Elmer Stricklett
Hooks Wiltse	NY	Jul 4, 1908	1-0	0	6	0	PHI	George McQuillan
Nap Rucker	BKN	Sep 5, 1908	6-0	0	14	3	BOS	Patsy Flaherty
Red Ames	NY	Apr 15, 1909	0-3	2	9	0	BKN	Kaiser Wilhelm
Jeff Tesreau	NY	Sep 6, 1912	3-0	2	2	2	PHI	Eppa Rixey
George Davis	BOS	Sep 9, 1914	7-0	5	4	2	PHI	Ben Tincup
Rube Marquard	NY	Apr 15, 1915	2-0	2	2	1	BKN	Nap Rucker
Jimmy Lavender	CHI	Aug 31, 1915	2-0	1	8	1	NY	Rube Schauer
Tom Hughes	BOS	Jun 16, 1916	2-0	2	3	0	PIT	Erv Kantlehner
Fred Toney	CIN	May 2, 1917	1-0	2	3	0	CHI	Hippo Vaughn
Hippo Vaughn	CHI	May 2, 1917	0-1	2	10	2	CIN	Fred Toney
Hod Eller	CIN	May 11, 1919	6-0	3	8	0	STL	Jakie May
Jesse Barnes	NY	May 7, 1922	6-0	1	5	0	PHI	Lee Meadows
Jesse Haines	STL	Jul 17, 1924	5-0	3	5	2	BOS	Tim McNamara
Dazzy Vance	BKN	Sep 13, 1925	10-1	1	9	3	PHI	Clarence Mitchell
Carl Hubbell	NY	May 8, 1929	11-0	1	4	3	PIT	Jesse Petty
Paul Dean	STL	Sep 21, 1934	3-0	1	6	0	BKN	Ray Benge
Johnny Vander Meer	CIN	Jun 11, 1938	3-0	3	4	0	BOS	Danny MacFayden
	CIN	Jun 15, 1938	6-0	8	7	0	BKN	Max Butcher
Tex Carleton	BKN	May 30, 1940	3-0	2	4	3	CIN	Jim Turner
Lon Warneke	STL	Aug 30, 1941	2-0	1	2	2	CIN	Elmer Riddle
Jim Tobin	BOS	Apr 27, 1944	2-0	2	6	0	BKN	Fritz Ostermueller
Clyde Shoun	CIN	May 15, 1944	1-0	1	1	0	BOS	Jim Tobin
Ed Head	BKN	Apr 23, 1946	5-0	3	2	1	BOS	Mort Cooper
Ewell Blackwell	CIN	Jun 18, 1947	6-0	4	3	0	BOS	Ed Wright
Rex Barney	BKN	Sep 9, 1948	2-0	3	4	2	NY	Monte Kennedy
Vern Bickford	BOS	Aug 11, 1950	7-0	4	3	0	BKN	Carl Erskine
Cliff Chambers	PIT	May 6, 1951	3-0	8	4	0	BOS	George Estock
Carl Erskine	BKN	Jun 19, 1952	5-0	1	1	0	CHI	Warren Hacker
Jim Wilson	MIL	Jun 12, 1954	2-0	2	6	0	PHI	Robin Roberts

PITCHING RECORDS

No-Hitters, NL (continued)

Player	Team	Date	Score	BB	SO	E	Opp.	Opp. Pitcher
Sam Jones	CHI	May 12, 1955	4-0	7	6	0	PIT	Nellie King
Carl Erskine	BKN	May 12, 1956	3-0	2	3	0	NY	Al Worthington
Sal Maglie	BKN	Sep 25, 1956	5-0	2	3	0	PHI	Jack Meyer
Harvey Haddix	PIT	May 26, 1959	0-1	1	8	0	MIL	Lew Burdette
Don Cardwell	CHI	May 15, 1960	4-0	1	7	0	STL	Lindy McDaniel
Lew Burdette	MIL	Aug 18, 1960	1-0	0	3	0	PHI	Gene Conley
Warren Spahn	MIL	Sep 16, 1960	4-0	2	15	0	PHI	John Buzhardt
	MIL	Apr 28, 1961	1-0	2	9	0	SF	Sam Jones
Sandy Koufax	LA	Jun 30, 1962	5-0	5	13	0	NY	Bob Miller
	LA	May 11, 1963	8-0	2	4	0	SF	Juan Marichal
Don Nottebart	HOU	May 17, 1963	4-1	3	8	1	PHI	Jack Hamilton
Juan Marichal	SF	Jun 15, 1963	1-0	2	5	0	HOU	Dick Drott
Ken Johnson	HOU	Apr 23, 1964	0-1	2	9	2	CIN	Joe Nuxhall
Sandy Koufax	LA	Jun 4, 1964	3-0	1	10	0	PHI	Chris Short
Jim Bunning	PHI	Jun 21, 1964	6-0	0	10	0	NY	Tracy Stallard
Jim Maloney	CIN	Jun 14, 1965	0-1	1	18	0	NY	Larry Bearnarth
	CIN	Aug 19, 1965	1-0	10	12	1	CHI	Larry Jackson
Sandy Koufax	LA	Sep 9, 1965	1-0	0	14	0	CHI	Bob Hendley
Don Wilson	HOU	Jun 18, 1967	2-0	3	15	0	ATL	Phil Niekro
George Culver	CIN	Jul 29, 1968	6-1	5	4	3	PHI	Chris Short
Gaylord Perry	SF	Sep 17, 1968	1-0	2	9	1	STL	Bob Gibson
Ray Washburn	STL	Sep 18, 1968	2-0	5	8	0	SF	Bobby Bolin
Bill Stoneman	MON	Apr 17, 1969	7-0	5	8	0	PHI	Jerry Johnson
Jim Maloney	CIN	Apr 30, 1969	10-0	5	13	0	HOU	Wade Blasingame
Don Wilson	HOU	May 1, 1969	4-0	6	15	1	CIN	Jim Merritt
Ken Holtzman	CHI	Aug 19, 1969	3-0	3	0	0	ATL	Phil Niekro
Bob Moose	PIT	Sep 20, 1969	4-0	3	6	0	NY	Gary Gentry
Dock Ellis	PIT	Jun 12, 1970	2-0	8	6	0	SD	Dave A. Roberts
Bill Singer	LA	Jul 20, 1970	5-0	0	10	2	PHI	Woody Fryman
Ken Holtzman	CHI	Jun 3, 1971	1-0	4	6	0	CIN	Gary Nolan
Rick Wise	PHI	Jun 23, 1971	4-0	1	3	0	CIN	Ross Grimsley
Bob Gibson	STL	Aug 14, 1971	11-0	3	10	0	PIT	Bob Johnson
Burt Hooton	CHI	Apr 16, 1972	4-0	7	7	0	PHI	Dick Selma
Milt Pappas	CHI	Sep 2, 1972	8-0	1	6	0	SD	Mike Caldwell
Bill Stoneman	MON	Oct 2, 1972	7-0	7	9	1	NY	Jim McAndrew
Phil Niekro	ATL	Aug 5, 1973	9-0	3	4	2	SD	Steve Arlin
Ed Halicki	SF	Aug 24, 1975	6-0	2	10	1	NY	Craig Swan
Larry Dierker	HOU	Jul 9, 1976	6-0	4	8	0	MON	Don Stanhouse
John Candelaria	PIT	Aug 9, 1976	2-0	1	7	2	LA	Doug Rau
John Montefusco	SF	Sep 29, 1976	9-0	1	4	0	ATL	Jamie Easterly
Bob Forsch	STL	Apr 16, 1978	5-0	2	3	1	PHI	Randy Lerch
Tom Seaver	CIN	Jun 16, 1978	4-0	3	3	1	STL	John Denny
Ken Forsch	HOU	Apr 7, 1979	6-0	2	5	0	ATL	Larry McWilliams
Jerry Reuss	LA	Jun 27, 1980	8-0	0	2	1	SF	Vida Blue

The scoreboard tells the whole story as **Don Larsen** throws his perfect game against the Dodgers in the 1956 World Series *(opposite page)*.

In the history of baseball, only 11 perfect games have been pitched, including the most famous of them all, Don Larsen's perfect game against the Dodgers in the 1956 World Series. A pitcher is credited with a perfect game when he retires all 27 batters he faces in a nine-inning game. That's why Harvey Haddix is credited with a perfect game, even though he gave up a hit and lost his perfect game, 1–0, in the thirteenth inning. Haddix retired 36 straight batters—12 perfect innings—before allowing a base runner.

One pitcher is credited with a perfect game even though he didn't start it. On June 23, 1917, Ernie Shore came in to pitch in the first inning with a runner on first and nobody out. Babe Ruth, the Red Sox starting pitcher, had just been thrown out of the game for arguing with umpire Brick Owen over a called fourth ball to the first hitter. In came Shore, without warming up. The runner tried to steal second and was thrown out. Shore then retired the next 26 hitters for a unique perfect game in relief.

Perfect Games

Player	Team	Date	Score	SO	Opp.	Opp. Pitcher
Lee Richmond	WOR N	Jun 12, 1880	1-0	7	CLE	Jim McCormick
Monte Ward	PRO N	Jun 17, 1880	5-0	7	BUF	Pud Galvin
Cy Young	BOS A	May 5, 1904	3-0	8	PHI	Rube Waddell
Addie Joss	CLE A	Oct 2, 1908	1-0	3	CHI	Ed Walsh
Ernie Shore	BOS A	Jun 23, 1917	4-0	2	WAS	Doc Ayers
Charlie Robertson	CHI A	Apr 30, 1922	2-0	6	DET	Herman Pillette
Don Larsen	NY A	Oct 8, 1956	2-0	7	BKN	Sal Maglie
Harvey Haddix	PIT N	May 26, 1959	0-1	8	MIL	Lew Burdette
Jim Bunning	PHI N	Jun 21, 1964	6-0	10	NY	Tracy Stallard
Sandy Koufax	LA N	Sep 9, 1965	1-0	14	CHI	Bob Hendley
Catfish Hunter	OAK A	May 8, 1968	4-0	11	MIN	Dave Boswell

Most No-Hitters, Career

Player	Team	Date	Score	Opp.
Sandy Koufax	LA N	Jun 30, 1962	5-0	NY
	LA N	May 11, 1963	8-0	SF
	LA N	Jun 4, 1964	3-0	PHI
	LA N	Sep 9, 1965	1-0	CHI
Nolan Ryan	CAL A	May 15, 1973	3-0	KC
	CAL A	Jul 15, 1973	6-0	DET
	CAL A	May 20, 1974	4-0	DET
	CAL A	Jun 1, 1975	1-0	BAL
Larry Corcoran	CHI N	Aug 19, 1880	6-0	BOS
	CHI N	Sep 20, 1882	5-0	WOR
	CHI N	Jun 27, 1884	6-0	PRO
Cy Young	CLE N	Sep 18, 1897	6-0	CIN
	BOS A	May 4, 1904	3-0	PHI
	BOS A	Jun 30, 1908	8-0	NY
Bob Feller	CLE A	Apr 16, 1940	1-0	CHI
	CLE A	Apr 30, 1946	1-0	NY
	CLE A	Jul 1, 1951	2-1	DET
Jim Maloney	CIN N	Jun 14, 1965	0-1	NY
	CIN N	Aug 9, 1965	1-0	CHI
	CIN N	Apr 30, 1969	1-0	HOU

Best Won-Lost Record, Season, AL (20 or more wins)

Player	Team		W	L	Pct.
Ron Guidry	NY	1978	25	3	.893
Lefty Grove	PHI	1931	31	4	.886
Joe Wood	BOS	1912	34	5	.872
Wild Bill Donovan	DET	1907	25	4	.862
Whitey Ford	NY	1961	25	4	.862
Lefty Grove	PHI	1930	28	5	.848
Lefty Gomez	NY	1934	26	5	.839
Denny McLain	DET	1968	31	6	.838
Walter Johnson	WAS	1913	36	7	.837
Spud Chandler	NY	1943	20	4	.833
Chief Bender	PHI	1910	23	5	.821
Eddie Plank	PHI	1904	26	6	.813
General Crowder	STL	1928	21	5	.808
Bobo Newsom	DET	1940	21	5	.808
Ernie Bonham	NY	1942	21	5	.808
Dave McNally	BAL	1971	21	5	.808
Eddie Cicotte	CHI	1919	29	7	.806
Boo Ferriss	BOS	1946	25	6	.806
Stan Coveleski	WAS	1925	20	5	.800

No regular starting pitcher has ever gone through a full season without losing a game. Rube Marquard of the Giants gave it a try in 1912, when he won his first 19 decisions, but he finished with a record of 26 wins and 11 losses.

Ron Guidry's percentage of .893 is the best won-lost percentage ever posted by a starter. The best won-lost percentage for a pitcher with at least 15 decisions belongs to Elroy Face, a reliever with the Pirates in the 1950s and 1960s, who was 18–1 in 1959 for a won-lost percentage of .947.

Tom Zachary of the New York Yankees, pitching in relief and as an occasional starter, won 12 games without a loss in 1929, the most wins ever by a pitcher in an undefeated season.

Best Won-Lost Record, Season, NL (20 or more wins)

Player	Team		W	L	Pct.
Preacher Roe	BKN	1951	22	3	.880
King Cole	CHI	1910	20	4	.833
Sandy Koufax	LA	1963	25	5	.833
Jack Chesbro	PIT	1902	28	6	.824
Dazzy Vance	BKN	1924	28	6	.824
Joe McGinnity	NY	1904	35	8	.814
Three Finger Brown	CHI	1906	26	6	.813
Carl Hubbell	NY	1936	26	6	.813
Dizzy Dean	STL	1934	30	7	.811
Harry Camnitz	PIT	1909	25	6	.806
Christy Mathewson	NY	1909	25	6	.806
Juan Marichal	SF	1966	25	6	.806
Sam Leever	PIT	1905	20	5	.800
Don Newcombe	BKN	1955	20	5	.800
John Candelaria	PIT	1977	20	5	.800

Ron Guidry, the Yankees' ace lefthander. His 25 wins in 1978 included a victory in the one-game play-off against the Red Sox.

PITCHING RECORDS

Worst Won-Lost Record, Season (12 or more losses)

Player	Team		W	L	Pct.	ERA
Steve Gerkin	PHI A	1945	0	12	.000	3.62
Russ Miller	PHI N	1928	0	12	.000	5.42
Jack Nabors	PHI A	1916	1	19	.050	3.47
Tom Sheehan	PHI A	1916	1	16	.059	3.69
Howie Judson	CHI A	1949	1	14	.067	4.54
Guy Morton	CLE A	1914	1	13	.071	3.02
Roy Moore	PHI A	1920	1	13	.071	4.68
Steve Hargan	CLE A	1971	1	13	.071	6.21
Troy Herriage	KC A	1956	1	13	.071	6.64
George Gill	DET A	1939				
	STL A	1939	1	13	.071	7.21
Carl Scheib	PHI A	1951	1	12	.077	4.47
Bob Miller	NY N	1962	1	12	.077	4.89
Wally Hebert	STL A	1932	1	12	.077	6.48
Jim Walkup	STL A	1938	1	12	.077	6.80

Twenty Wins and 20 Losses in Same Year, AL

Player	Team		W	L
Joe McGinnity	BAL	1901	26	21
Bill Dinneen	BOS	1902	21	21
George Mullin	DET	1905	21	20
	DET	1907	20	20
Jim Scott	CHI	1913	20	20
Walter Johnson	WAS	1916	25	20
Wilbur Wood	CHI	1973	24	20

Twenty Wins and 20 Losses in Same Year, NL

Player	Team		W	L
Joe McGinnity	NY	1903	31	20
Irv Young	BOS	1906	20	21
Phil Niekro	ATL	1979	21	20

Since 1900, only eight pitchers have won 20 or more games with a last-place team. Considering the quality of the team he pitched for, Steve Carlton's 1972 season might be the greatest ever turned in by a pitcher. Carlton won 27 and lost just 10; without Carlton, the Phillies were 32–87. He won 15 straight games in one stretch for a team that couldn't win one game in three without him. Carlton won a higher percentage of his team's wins than any other pitcher in history.

Twenty Wins with Last-Place Team, AL

Player	Team		W	L	Team W	Team L
Scott Perry	PHI	1918	21	19	52	76
Howard Ehmke	BOS	1923	20	17	61	91
Sloppy Thurston	CHI	1924	20	14	66	87
Ned Garver	STL	1951	20	12	52	102
Nolan Ryan	CAL	1974	22	16	68	94

Twenty Wins with Last-Place Team, NL

Player	Team		W	L	Team W	Team L
Noodles Hahn	CIN	1901	22	19	52	87
Steve Carlton	PHI	1972	27	10	59	97
Phil Niekro	ATL	1979	21	20	66	94

Phil Niekro, pitching for the Atlanta Braves. The durable Niekro has pitched more than 200 innings for 14 straight seasons.

PITCHING RECORDS

Thirty-Game Winners, AL

Player	Team		W	L	Pct.	ERA	IP	BB	SO	ShO
Jack Chesbro	NY	1904	41	12	.774	1.82	455	88	239	6
Ed Walsh	CHI	1908	40	15	.727	1.42	464	56	269	12
Walter Johnson	WAS	1913	36	7	.837	1.09	346	38	243	12
Joe Wood	BOS	1912	34	5	.872	1.91	344	82	258	10
Cy Young	BOS	1901	33	10	.767	1.62	371	36	119	4
	BOS	1902	32	10	.762	2.15	385	33	166	3
Walter Johnson	WAS	1912	32	12	.727	1.39	368	76	303	8
Lefty Grove	PHI	1931	31	4	.886	2.06	289	62	175	3
Denny McLain	DET	1968	31	6	.838	1.96	336	63	280	6
Jack Coombs	PHI	1910	31	9	.769	1.30	353	115	224	13
Jim Bagby	CLE	1920	31	12	.721	2.89	340	79	73	3

Thirty-Game Winners, NL since 1900

Player	Team		W	L	Pct.	ERA	IP	BB	SO	ShO
Christy Mathewson	NY	1908	37	11	.771	1.43	391	42	259	12
Joe McGinnity	NY	1904	35	8	.814	1.61	408	86	144	9
Christy Mathewson	NY	1904	33	12	.733	2.03	368	78	212	4
Grover Alexander	PHI	1916	33	12	.733	1.55	389	50	167	16
Christy Mathewson	NY	1905	31	8	.795	1.27	339	64	206	9
Grover Alexander	PHI	1915	31	10	.756	1.22	376	64	241	12
Joe McGinnity	NY	1903	31	20	.608	2.43	434	109	171	3
Dizzy Dean	STL	1934	30	7	.811	2.66	312	75	195	7
Grover Alexander	PHI	1917	30	13	.698	1.86	388	58	201	8
Christy Mathewson	NY	1903	30	13	.698	2.26	366	100	267	3

The 300-Win Club

Player	W	L	ERA	ShO	SO
Cy Young	511	313	2.63	77	2819
Walter Johnson	416	279	2.17	113	3503
Christy Mathewson	373	188	2.13	83	2511
Grover Alexander	373	208	2.56	91	2199
Warren Spahn	363	245	3.09	63	2583
Pud Galvin	361	309	2.87	56	1799
Kid Nichols	360	202	2.94	48	1885
Tim Keefe	344	225	2.83	40	2533
John Clarkson	327	177	2.81	37	1978
Eddie Plank	327	192	2.34	69	2261
Mickey Welch	311	207	2.71	40	1850
Old Hoss Radbourn	310	192	2.67	35	1830
Lefty Grove	300	140	3.06	32	2266
Early Wynn	300	244	3.54	49	2334

Cy Young—the very name *means* pitching. Young *(opposite page)* won 20 or more games every year from 1891 to 1904. His record of 511 wins and 753 complete games will never be equaled, or even approached. Young pitched a complete game in the first World Series game ever played. The annual award given to each league's best pitcher bears his name.

Winning 300 games is the same kind of standard for pitchers as 3,000 hits is for batters. But while seven players have reached the 3,000-hit level since 1970, no pitcher has won his three-hundredth game since Early Wynn did it in 1963.

It would take fifteen straight twenty-win seasons to reach the 300 mark. You'd expect a pitcher to have to start young and stay strong through his thirties to be able to win 300. One pitcher who didn't go about it that way was Warren Spahn. Spahn, the ace left-hander for the Boston and Milwaukee Braves, didn't win his first major league game until after he was twenty-five and once ran off six straight seasons of twenty or more wins—*beginning* when he was thirty-six. He ended his career with a total of 363 wins.

PITCHING RECORDS

Most Strikeouts, Season, AL

Player	Team		SO
Nolan Ryan	CAL	1973	383
	CAL	1974	367
Rube Waddell	PHI	1904	349
Bob Feller	CLE	1946	348
Nolan Ryan	CAL	1977	341
	CAL	1972	329
	CAL	1976	327
Sam McDowell	CLE	1965	325
Walter Johnson	WAS	1910	313
	WAS	1912	308
Mickey Lolich	DET	1971	308
Sam McDowell	CLE	1970	304
Rube Waddell	PHI	1903	301
Vida Blue	OAK	1971	301
Rube Waddell	PHI	1905	287
Sam McDowell	CLE	1968	283
Denny McLain	DET	1968	280
Sam McDowell	CLE	1969	279
Hal Newhouser	DET	1946	275
Mickey Lolich	DET	1969	271
Ed Walsh	CHI	1908	269
Frank Tanana	CAL	1975	269
Luis Tiant	CLE	1968	264
Herb Score	CLE	1956	263
Bob Feller	CLE	1940	261
Frank Tanana	CAL	1976	261
Bob Feller	CLE	1941	260
Nolan Ryan	CAL	1978	260
Ed Walsh	CHI	1910	258
Joe Wood	BOS	1912	258
Bert Blyleven	MIN	1973	258
Ed Walsh	CHI	1911	255
	CHI	1912	254
Mickey Lolich	DET	1972	250

Most Strikeouts, Season, NL

Player	Team		SO
Sandy Koufax	LA	1965	382
	LA	1966	317
J. R. Richard	HOU	1979	313
Steve Carlton	PHI	1972	310
Sandy Koufax	LA	1963	306
J. R. Richard	HOU	1978	303
Tom Seaver	NY	1971	289
Steve Carlton	PHI	1980	286
Tom Seaver	NY	1970	283
Bob Veale	PIT	1965	275
Ferguson Jenkins	CHI	1970	274
Bob Gibson	STL	1970	274
Ferguson Jenkins	CHI	1969	273
Bob Gibson	STL	1965	270
	STL	1969	269
Sandy Koufax	LA	1961	269
Jim Bunning	PHI	1965	268
Bob Gibson	STL	1968	268
Christy Mathewson	NY	1903	267
Jim Maloney	CIN	1963	265
Ferguson Jenkins	CHI	1971	263
Dazzy Vance	BKN	1924	262
Phil Niekro	ATL	1977	262
Ferguson Jenkins	CHI	1968	260
Christy Mathewson	NY	1908	259
Jim Bunning	PHI	1967	253
	PHI	1966	252
Bill Stoneman	MON	1971	251
Don Drysdale	LA	1963	251
Tom Seaver	NY	1973	251
Bob Veale	PIT	1964	250

A strikeout gives a pitcher the same kind of thrill that a batter gets from hitting a home run. It's a clear victory in the battle between pitcher and hitter. The great fastball pitchers throw pitches that blow past a batter like a speeding locomotive. Walter Johnson was nicknamed "The Big Train"; Nolan Ryan's fastball has been called "Ryan's Express."

Working with nothing but a blazing fastball, Walter Johnson struck out a total of 3,508 batters. His record has stood for over 50 years, but Nolan Ryan seems likely to break it. Going into the 1981 season, Ryan was 399 strikeouts shy of Johnson's mark. Johnson needed 21 seasons to reach his total; the 1981 season is Ryan's fifteenth. Ryan and Sandy Koufax are the only pitchers with more strikeouts than innings pitched.

It's true, however, that batters didn't strike out as often in Johnson's day. During Johnson's career, teams averaged fewer than four strikeouts a game. Today, the average is closer to six.

Most Strikeouts, Career

Player	SO	Player	SO
Walter Johnson	3508	Don Sutton	2652
Gaylord Perry	3276	Warren Spahn	2583
Bob Gibson	3117	Bob Feller	2581
Nolan Ryan	3109	Phil Niekro	2578
Tom Seaver	2988	Tim Keefe	2533
Steve Carlton	2969	Christy Mathewson	2511
Ferguson Jenkins	2899	Don Drysdale	2486
Jim Bunning	2855	Sam McDowell	2453
Mickey Lolich	2832	Jim Kaat	2400
Cy Young	2804	Sandy Koufax	2396

Nolan Ryan rears back to fire his overpowering fastball, which has been timed at more than 100 miles per hour.

Most Strikeouts in Nine-Inning Game, AL

Player	Team	Date	SO	Opp.
Nolan Ryan	CAL	Aug 12, 1974	19	BOS
Bob Feller	CLE	Oct 2, 1938	18	DET
Nolan Ryan	CAL	Sep 10, 1976	18	CHI
Ron Guidry	NY	Jun 17, 1978	18	CAL
Bob Feller	CLE	Sep 13, 1936	17	PHI
Bill Monbouquette	BOS	May 12, 1961	17	WAS
Nolan Ryan	CAL	Sep 30, 1972	17	MIN
	CAL	May 17, 1973	17	DET
Mickey Lolich	DET	Jun 17, 1973	17	MIN
Frank Tanana	CAL	Jun 21, 1975	17	TEX
Rube Waddell	STL	Jul 27, 1908	16	PHI
	STL	Jul 29, 1908	16	PHI
Bob Feller	CLE	Sep 7, 1936	16	STL
	CLE	Aug 25, 1937	16	BOS
Jack Harshman	CHI	Jul 25, 1954	16	BOS
Herb Score	CLE	May 1, 1955	16	BOS
Luis Tiant	CLE	Aug 22, 1967	16	CAL
Sam McDowell	CLE	May 1, 1968	16	CAL
Luis Tiant	CLE	Sep 9, 1968	16	MIN
Mickey Lolich	DET	May 23, 1969	16	CAL
	DET	Jun 9, 1969	16	SEA
Nolan Ryan	CAL	Jul 1, 1972	16	OAK
	CAL	Jul 9, 1972	16	BOS
Rudy May	CAL	Aug 10, 1972	16	MIN
Nolan Ryan	CAL	Sep 27, 1973	16	MIN
	CAL	Jun 9, 1979	16	DET

Steve Carlton *(opposite page),* then with the Cardinals, tied an 85-year-old record when he struck out 19 batters in a nine-inning game. **Bob Feller** *(left)* was just nineteen years old when he struck out a then-record 18 AL batters on October 2, 1938.

Most Strikeouts in Nine-Inning Game, NL

Player	Team	Date	SO	Opp.
Charlie Sweeney	PRO	Jun 7, 1884	19	BOS
Steve Carlton	STL	Sep 15, 1969	19	NY
Tom Seaver	NY	Apr 22, 1970	19	SD
Sandy Koufax	LA	Aug 31, 1959	18	SF
	LA	Apr 24, 1962	18	CHI
Don Wilson	HOU	Jul 14, 1968	18	CIN
Bill Gullickson	MON	Sep 10, 1980	18	NY
Dizzy Dean	STL	Jul 30, 1933	17	CHI
Art Mahaffey	PHI	Apr 29, 1961	17	CHI
John Clarkson	CHI	Aug 18, 1886	16	KC
Frank Gilmore	WAS	Sep 28, 1886	16	STL
Noodles Hahn	CIN	May 22, 1901	16	BOS
Joe Corbett	STL	Apr 18, 1904	16	CHI
Christy Mathewson	NY	Oct 8, 1904	16	STL
Nap Rucker	BKN	Jul 24, 1909	16	PIT
Rube Marquard	NY	May 13, 1910	16	STL
Sandy Koufax	LA	Jun 22, 1959	16	PHI
	LA	May 26, 1962	16	PHI
Jim Maloney	CIN	May 21, 1963	16	MIL
Bob Veale	PIT	Jun 1, 1965	16	PHI
Steve Carlton	STL	Sep 26, 1967	16	PHI
Don Wilson	HOU	Sep 10, 1968	16	CIN
Steve Carlton	STL	May 21, 1970	16	PHI
Bob Gibson	STL	May 23, 1970	16	PHI
Nolan Ryan	NY	May 29, 1971	16	SD
Tom Seaver	NY	May 28, 1973	16	SF

Four strikeouts in one inning? Yes, four strikeouts. Generally, the catcher has to hold onto the third strike for the batter to be out. That's why a catcher is credited with a putout on a strikeout. If he drops the ball, the batter can try to run down to first, and the catcher must either tag him or throw down to the first baseman. (If there's a man on first and less than two out, the batter is out even if the ball is dropped. This stops the catcher from dropping the ball on purpose to try for a quick double play.)

When a batter reaches base on a passed ball or wild pitch, the pitcher is given credit for a strikeout, but the batter is safe, and the pitcher still has to get three outs to retire the side. The pitchers listed below all struck out the side and had a batter reach base on a dropped third strike in the same inning. That makes an "impossible" total of four strikeouts!

Four Strikeouts in One Inning, AL

Player	Team	Date	Inn.	Opp.	Opp. Batters
Walter Johnson	WAS	Apr 15, 1911	5	BOS	Ray Collins
					Larry Gardner
					Harry Hooper
					Duffy Lewis
Guy Morton	CLE	Jun 11, 1916	6	PHI	Whitey Witt
					Charlie Pick
					Nap Lajoie
					Stuffy McInnis
Ryne Duren	LA	May 18, 1961	7	CHI	Minnie Minoso
					Roy Sievers
					J. C. Martin
					Sammy Esposito
Lee Stange	CLE	Sep 2, 1964	7	WAS	Don Lock
					Willie Kirkland
					Mike Brumley
					Don Zimmer
Mike Cuellar	BAL	May 29, 1970	4	CAL	Alex Johnson
					Ken McMullen
					Tommie Reynolds
					Jim Spencer
Mike Paxton	CLE	Jul 21, 1978	5	SEA	Bruce Bochte
					Tom Paciorek
					Dan Meyer
					Bill Stein

Four Strikeouts in One Inning, NL

Player	Team	Date	Inn.	Opp.	Opp. Batters
Cannonball Crane	NY	Oct 4, 1888	5	CHI	Fred Pfeffer Ned Williamson Tom Burns John Tener
Hooks Wiltse	NY	May 15, 1906	5	CIN	Jim Delahanty Tommy Corcoran Admiral Schlei Chick Fraser
Jim Davis	CHI	May 27, 1956	6	STL	Hal Smith Jackie Brandt Lindy McDaniel Don Blasingame
Joe Nuxhall	CIN	Aug 11, 1959	6	MIL	Eddie Mathews Joe Adcock Del Crandall Johnny Logan
Pete Richert	LA	Apr 12, 1962	3	CIN	Frank Robinson Gordy Coleman Wally Post Johnny Edwards
Don Drysdale	LA	Apr 17, 1965	2	PHI	Wes Covington Tony Gonzalez Dick Stuart Clay Dalrymple
Bob Gibson	STL	Jun 7, 1965	4	PIT	Jerry Lynch Jim Pagliaroni Bill Mazeroski Del Crandall
Bill Bonham	CHI	Jul 31, 1974	2	MON	Mike Torrez Ron Hunt Tim Foli Willie Davis
Phil Niekro	ATL	Jul 29, 1977	6	PIT	Dave Parker Bill Robinson Rennie Stennett Omar Moreno

PITCHING RECORDS

Perfect Innings, AL (3 strikeouts on 9 pitches)

Player	Team	Date	Inn.	Opp.
Rube Waddell	PHI	Jul 1, 1902	3	BAL
Sloppy Thurston	CHI	Aug 22, 1923	12	PHI
Lefty Grove	PHI	Aug 23, 1928	2	CLE
	PHI	Sep 27, 1928	7	CHI
Jim Bunning	DET	Aug 2, 1959	9	BOS
Al Downing	NY	Aug 11, 1967	2	CLE
Nolan Ryan	CAL	Jul 9, 1972	2	BOS

Perfect Innings, NL (3 strikeouts on 9 pitches)

Player	Team	Date	Inn.	Opp.
Hod Eller	CIN	Aug 21, 1917	9	NY
Joe Oeschger	BOS	Sep 8, 1921	4	PHI
Dazzy Vance	BKN	Sep 14, 1924	3	CHI
Sandy Koufax	LA	Jun 30, 1962	1	PHI
	LA	Apr 18, 1964	3	CIN
Bob Bruce	HOU	Apr 19, 1964	8	STL
Nolan Ryan	NY	Apr 19, 1968	3	PIT
Bob Gibson	STL	May 12, 1969	7	LA
Lynn McGlothen	STL	Aug 19, 1975	2	CIN
Bruce Sutter	CHI	Jul 8, 1977	9	STL

Rube Waddell helped establish the tradition of crazy, unpredictable left-handed pitchers. Waddell drank, chased fire engines, and occasionally disappeared for days at a time, but when he was ready to pitch, there were few better.

The Years of Change: 1940–1959

Baseball fans could be forgiven if they were distracted by off-field events that had a greater effect on the game than anything accomplished on the field. Able-bodied ballplayers were called into military service in World War II, leaving the game to be played by the overaged and the undertalented.

The war interrupted the careers of many great ballplayers. Ted Williams probably suffered the most, missing three whole years during World War II and most of two others during the Korean War. Had he not lost those years, Williams would surely have reached the 3,000-hit plateau and been the first man since Babe Ruth to hit over 600 homers. Similarly, Bob Feller, who appeared in only nine games from 1942 to 1945, might well have picked up the 1,000 additional strikeouts he would have needed to break Walter Johnson's career record.

In 1947, Jackie Robinson made his debut with the Brooklyn Dodgers and became the first black player in the major leagues. The long-delayed acceptance of black ballplayers put an end to the old Negro Leagues, the all-black teams that toured the country, often playing in major league ball parks when the big league teams were on the road.

For fifty years, no team in baseball had moved its home from one city to another. Then the Braves left Boston and moved to Milwaukee in 1953, where they set a new attendance record. Encouraged by the Braves' success, the St. Louis Browns became the Baltimore Orioles, and the Philadelphia Athletics moved to Kansas City. But the most unsettling move came at the end of the 1957 season, when the Brooklyn Dodgers and New York Giants took their bitter crosstown rivalry to Los Angeles and San Francisco, respectively. The move ended the golden era of baseball in New York: In the twelve years since the end of World War II, there had been seven all-New York "subway" World Series.

On the field, the Yankees were even more dominant than before. They captured thirteen pennants, winning ten of twelve from 1947 to 1958, and ten World Series, including an unprecedented five in a row. Yankee manager Casey Stengel, "The Old Professor," mastered the art of platooning—pitting left-handed batters against right-handed pitchers and right-handed batters against left-handed pitchers.

The period featured many great individual achievements, including Joe DiMaggio's 56-game hitting streak and Ted Williams's .406 average, both in 1941. But the greatest single accomplishment was by a Yankee pitcher with a lifetime won-lost record ten games below .500, who had given up four runs in 1⅔ innings just three days earlier. Don Larsen needed just 97 pitches to retire 27 consecutive batters as he pitched the only no-hitter in World Series' history, a perfect game against the 1956 Dodgers.

WARTIME BASEBALL

While Ted Williams *(left)* and many other stars enlisted in the armed forces during World War II, baseball carried on with men who were either physically unfit for military service or were too young to be drafted. The symbol of wartime baseball is one-armed outfielder Pete Gray *(below)*, who played in 77 games for the St. Louis Browns in 1945. Gray would field the ball in the glove he held in his left hand, then drop the glove and throw the ball in with his bare hand. Swinging the bat with one hand, he hit .218 in his brief career.

BREAKING THROUGH

In 1885, Cap Anson drew the color line that kept black players out of the major leagues. Black ballplayers were forced to play in the Negro Leagues, traveling around the country playing in big league parks one day, on vacant sandlots the next. One of the best of these teams was the Kansas City Monarchs. Their ace pitcher, Leroy "Satchel" Paige *(far left, with Jackie Robinson),* is considered one of the greatest all-time pitchers by such stars as Joe DiMaggio and Dizzy Dean, who played against him in exhibitions. The color barrier fell in 1947, when Brooklyn Dodger general manager Branch Rickey signed infielder Jackie Robinson *(below, with Rickey).* Fans taunted Robinson, and opponents deliberately spiked him, but Robinson stood up to the abuse without ever losing his temper. His courage under pressure paved the way for a generation of black ballplayers. Paige finally made it to the majors in 1948, when he was 42 years old (although some insist he was really as much as 10 years older).

DIMAGGIO AND WILLIAMS

"The Yankee Clipper" and "The Splendid Splinter," Joe DiMaggio and Ted Williams were rivals throughout the late 1930s and 1940s. Their individual battles mirrored the intense rivalry between their two teams, the Yankees and the Red Sox. DiMaggio *(above)* was a smooth, graceful centerfielder who flowed across the field with long, effortless strides. He was named AL Most Valuable Player three times in his 13-year career. Williams, a leftfielder, was the more intense figure of the two *(opposite page, top)*. He was a left-handed hitter who pulled the ball with great power, even against defenses which placed six men—all four infielders and two outfielders—to the right of second base. Williams paid an appropriate farewell to his fans at Boston's Fenway Park on September 26, 1960—he hit a home run in his last at bat in the majors.

JACKIE ROBINSON

Branch Rickey studied many black players before choosing Jackie Robinson to break the color barrier. It was important that the first black major leaguer be such a great player that his teammates would have to accept him. Robinson fit the role perfectly. A great natural athlete, Robinson had been an all-American football player and track star at UCLA. He was a fine fielder and hitter, but he particularly shone on the basepaths. He was a daring, aggressive base-runner in a time when the stolen base was a rarity. He stole home 19 times, the highest total since World War II.

The 1912 season was a banner year for pitching streaks. Rube Marquard won 19 straight games to start the season, and Walter Johnson and Smokey Joe Wood set the AL record with 16 straight wins each. Robert Moses "Lefty" Grove tied the record in 1931 and can hardly be blamed for not breaking it. His streak was snapped when he lost a 1–0 decision, the only run coming as a result of the left-fielder's error.

If we stretch the definition of streaks to include those that ran across two seasons, then the longest streak ever was turned in by Carl Hubbell, the great screwball pitcher for the New York Giants. Hubbell, who struck out Babe Ruth, Lou Gehrig, Jimmie Foxx, Al Simmons, and Joe Cronin in succession during the 1934 All-Star Game, won his last 16 decisions in 1936 and his first eight in 1937, a total of 24 consecutive wins. The record for a relief pitcher belongs to Elroy Face, who won his last five games in 1958 and his first 17 in 1959 for a total of 22.

Most Consecutive Wins, AL

Player	Team		W	Player	Team		W
Walter Johnson	WAS	1912	16	Ellis Kinder	BOS	1949	13
Joe Wood	BOS	1912	16	Dave McNally	BAL	1971	13
Lefty Grove	PHI	1931	16	Catfish Hunter	OAK	1973	13
Schoolboy Rowe	DET	1934	16	Ron Guidry	NY	1978	13
General Crowder	WAS	1932	15	Cy Young	BOS	1901	12
Johnny Allen	CLE	1937	15	Russ Ford	NY	1910	12
Dave McNally	BAL	1969	15	Walter Johnson	WAS	1924	12
Gaylord Perry	CLE	1974	15	Tom Zachary	NY	1929	12
Jack Chesbro	NY	1904	14	George Earnshaw	PHI	1931	12
Walter Johnson	WAS	1913	14	Johnny Allen	CLE	1938	12
Chief Bender	PHI	1914	14	Atley Donald	NY	1939	12
Lefty Grove	PHI	1928	14	Boo Ferriss	BOS	1946	12
Whitey Ford	NY	1961	14	Tex Hughson	BOS	1946	12
Steve Stone	BAL	1980	14	Jack Kramer	BOS	1948	12
Dutch Leonard	BOS	1914	13	Luis Arroyo	NY	1961	12
Stan Coveleski	WAS	1925	13	Whitey Ford	NY	1963	12
Wes Ferrell	CLE	1930	13	Dave McNally	BAL	1968	12
Bobo Newsom	DET	1940	13	Pat Dobson	BAL	1971	12

Most Consecutive Wins, NL

Player	Team		W	Player	Team		W
Tim Keefe	NY	1888	19	Larry Corcoran	CHI	1880	13
Rube Marquard	NY	1912	19	Charlie Buffinton	BOS	1884	13
Old Hoss Radbourn	PRO	1884	18	Cy Young	CLE	1892	13
Mickey Welch	NY	1885	17	Frank Dwyer	CIN	1896	13
Pat Luby	CHI	1890	17	Christy Mathewson	NY	1909	13
Roy Face	PIT	1959	17	Deacon Phillippe	PIT	1910	13
Jim McCormick	CHI	1886	16	Burleigh Grimes	NY	1927	13
Carl Hubbell	NY	1936	16	Brooks Lawrence	CIN	1956	13
Ewell Blackwell	CIN	1947	16	Phil Regan	LA	1966	13
Jack Sanford	SF	1962	16	Dock Ellis	PIT	1971	13
Dazzy Vance	BKN	1924	15	John Clarkson	CHI	1885	12
Bob Gibson	STL	1968	15	Charlie Ferguson	PHI	1886	12
Steve Carlton	PHI	1972	15	Jack Chesbro	PIT	1902	12
Jim McCormick	CHI	1885	14	Hooks Wiltse	NY	1904	12
Jocko Flynn	CHI	1886	14	Ed Reulbach	CHI	1906	12
Joe McGinnity	NY	1904	14	Dick Rudolph	BOS	1914	12
Ed Reulbach	CHI	1909	14	Burt Hooton	LA	1975	12

Rube Marquard of the New York Giants began the 1912 season by streaking to a 19–0 record before picking up his first loss.

PITCHING RECORDS

Most Consecutive Losses, AL

Player	Team		L	Player	Team		L
Bob Groom	WAS	1909	19	Roy Moore	PHI	1920	13
Jack Nabors	PHI	1916	19	Dutch Henry	CHI	1930	13
Mike Parrott	SEA	1980	16	Lum Harris	PHI	1943	13
Joe Harris	BOS	1906	14	Red Ruffing	BOS	1929	12
Howie Judson	CHI	1949	14	Walt Masterson	WAS	1940	12
Paul Calvert	WAS	1949	14	Bobo Newsom	PHI	1945	12
Matt Keough	OAK	1979	14	Steve Gerkin	PHI	1945	12
Bill Carrick	WAS	1901	13	Charlie Bishop	PHI	1953	12
Guy Morton	CLE	1914	13				

Most Consecutive Losses, NL

Player	Team		L	Player	Team		L
Cliff Curtis	BOS	1910	18	Dutch McCall	CHI	1948	13
Roger Craig	NY	1963	18	Blondie Purcell	CIN	1880	12
Dory Dean	CIN	1876	16	John Coleman	PHI	1883	12
Sam Weaver	MIL	1878	16	Henry Thielman	CIN	1902	12
Jim Hughey	CLE	1899	16	Mal Eason	BKN	1905	12
Craig Anderson	NY	1962	16	Rube Marquard	NY	1914	12
Frank Gilmore	WAS	1887	14	Pete Schneider	CIN	1914	12
Frank Bates	CLE	1899	14	Russ Miller	PHI	1928	12
Jim Pastorius	BKN	1908	14	Si Johnson	CIN	1933	12
Buster Brown	BOS	1911	14	Max Butcher	PHI		
Sam Moffet	CLE	1884	13		PIT	1939	12
Burleigh Grimes	PIT	1917	13	Hugh Mulcahy	PHI	1940	12
Joe Oeschger	BOS	1922	13	Bob Miller	NY	1962	12
Ben Cantwell	BOS	1935	13	Ken Reynolds	PHI	1972	12
Dick Barrett	PHI	1944	13				

PITCHING RECORDS

Most Consecutive Strikeouts, AL

Player	Team	Date	SO	Opp.
Nolan Ryan	CAL	Jul 9, 1972	8	BOS
	CAL	Jul 25, 1973	8	MIL
Walter Johnson	WAS	Jul 8, 1909	7	STL
Ryne Duren	LA	Jun 9, 1961	7	BOS
Denny McLain	DET	Jun 15, 1963	7	NY
Pete Richert	WAS	Apr 24, 1966	7	DET
Phil Ortega	WAS	May 29, 1966	7	BOS
Jim Merritt	MIN	Jul 21, 1966	7	WAS
Sammy Stewart	BAL	Sep 1, 1978	7	CLE
Wild Bill Donovan	DET	Sep 6, 1908	6	STL
Walter Johnson	WAS	Jul 22, 1912	6	DET
Buck O'Brien	BOS	Apr 25, 1913	6	WAS
Jim Scott	CHI	Jun 22, 1913	6	STL
Walter Johnson	WAS	May 23, 1924	6	DET
Lefty Gomez	NY	Jun 16, 1937	6	CLE
Bobo Newsom	STL	May 18, 1938	6	NY
Bob Feller	CLE	Oct 2, 1938	6	DET
Bob Kuzava	CHI	Aug 26, 1949	6	BOS
Whitey Ford	NY	Jul 20, 1956	6	KC
	NY	Jun 3, 1958	6	CHI
John Hiller	DET	Aug 6, 1968	6	CLE
Ray Culp	BOS	May 18, 1970	6	CAL
Bert Blyleven	MIN	Sep 16, 1970	6	CAL

Most Consecutive Strikeouts, NL

Player	Team	Date	SO	Opp.
Tom Seaver	NY	Apr 22, 1970	10	SD
Mickey Welch	NY	Aug 24, 1884	9	PIT
Charlie Buffinton	BOS	Sep 2, 1884	8	CLE
Max Surkont	MIL	May 25, 1953	8	CIN
Jim Maloney	CIN	May 21, 1963	8	MIL
Johnny Podres	LA	Jul 2, 1963	8	CIN
Hooks Wiltse	NY	May 5, 1906	7	CIN
Dazzy Vance	BKN	Aug 1, 1924	7	CHI
Van Mungo	BKN	Jun 25, 1936	7	CIN
Steve Renko	MON	Oct 3, 1972	7	NY
John Clarkson	CHI	1884	6	STL
Babe Adams	PIT	Sep 6, 1909	6	NY
Bob Keefe	CIN	Jun 20, 1911	6	STL
Rube Marquard	NY	Jul 12, 1911	6	PIT
Dizzy Dean	STL	Aug 14, 1932	6	CHI
Preacher Roe	BKN	Sep 5, 1948	6	NY
Ben Wade	BKN	May 7, 1952	6	PIT
Karl Spooner	BKN	Jul 22, 1954	6	NY
Jack Meyer	PHI	Sep 22, 1958	6	STL
Warren Spahn	MIL	Sep 16, 1960	6	PHI
Pete Richert	LA	Apr 12, 1962	6	STL

PITCHING RECORDS

Most Consecutive Strikeouts, NL (continued)

Player	Team	Date	SO	Opp.
Ron Perranoski	LA	Sep 12, 1966	6	STL
Dick Kelley	ATL	Sep 8, 1967	6	PHI
Joe Hoerner	STL	Jun 1, 1968	6	NY
Don Gullett	CIN	Aug 3, 1970	6	STL
Andy Messersmith	LA	May 28, 1973	6	PHI
Bruce Sutter	CHI	Sep 8, 1977	6	NY

The scorecard from **Tom Seaver's** record performance on April 22, 1970, when he struck out ten straight batters. The letter next to each "K" for strikeout indicates whether the batter struck out swinging (S) or on a called third strike (C).

The save has only recently been given a place in the baseball record book. Relief pitchers have been coming to the rescue of starters since the turn of the century, but official records weren't kept on saves until the 1960s. At that point, statisticians went back over the box scores of early games to give proper credit to old-time relievers.

What is a save? Rule 10.20 states that a pitcher who finishes a game won by his club but is not the winning pitcher gets credit for a save if he meets one of these three conditions:

1. He entered the game with a lead of no more than three runs and pitched for at least one inning;
2. He entered the game with the potential tying run on base, at bat, or waiting in the on-deck circle;
3. He pitches effectively for at least three innings. (This is up to the judgment of the official scorer.)

While there have always been a few great game-savers, the value of relief pitching wasn't widely recognized until 1950, when Phillies reliever Jim Konstanty became the first reliever ever to win the Most Valuable Player Award. Mike Marshall of the Dodgers became the first reliever to win the Cy Young Award in 1974, when he set the record by pitching in 104 games.

Most Saves, Season, AL

Player	Team		SV	Player	Team		SV
John Hiller	DET	1973	38	Terry Forster	CHI	1972	29
Sparky Lyle	NY	1972	35	Jim Kern	TEX	1979	29
Ron Perranoski	MIN	1970	34	Ellis Kinder	BOS	1953	27
Rich Gossage	NY	1980	33	Stu Miller	BAL	1963	27
Dan Quisenberry	KC	1980	33	Hoyt Wilhelm	CHI	1964	27
Jack Aker	KC	1966	32	Darold Knowles	WAS	1970	27
Mike Marshall	MIN	1979	32	Sparky Lyle	NY	1973	27
Ron Perranoski	MIN	1969	31	Rich Gossage	CHI	1975	27
Ken Sanders	MIL	1971	31		NY	1978	27
Bill Campbell	BOS	1977	31	Tim Stoddard	BAL	1980	26
Ed Farmer	CHI	1980	30	Lerrin LaGrow	CHI	1977	25
Luis Arroyo	NY	1961	29	Sparky Lyle	NY	1977	25
Lindy McDaniel	NY	1970	29	Dave LaRoche	CAL	1978	25

Most Saves, Season, NL

Player	Team		SV	Player	Team		SV
Clay Carroll	CIN	1972	37	Kent Tekulve	PIT	1978	31
Rollie Fingers	SD	1978	37		PIT	1979	31
Bruce Sutter	CHI	1979	37	Dave Giusti	PIT	1971	30
Wayne Granger	CIN	1970	35	Fred Gladding	HOU	1969	29
Rollie Fingers	SD	1977	35	Roy Face	PIT	1962	28
Ted Abernathy	CHI	1965	31	Ted Abernathy	CIN	1967	28
Mike Marshall	MON	1973	31	Doug Bair	CIN	1978	28
Bruce Sutter	CHI	1977	31	Wayne Granger	CIN	1969	27

Rollie Fingers holds the career record for saves. In 1977, while on the San Diego Padres, Fingers won or saved 43 of his team's 65 victories. Fingers grew his trademark handlebar mustache as part of a Mustache Day promotion for Oakland owner Charles O. Finley.

Most Saves, Season, NL (continued)

Player	Team		SV	Player	Team		SV
Cecil Upshaw	ATL	1969	27	Phil Regan	LA	1968	
Tug McGraw	NY	1972	27		CHI	1968	25
Bruce Sutter	CHI	1978	27	Tug McGraw	NY	1973	25
Lindy McDaniel	STL	1960	26	Gene Garber	PHI	1978	
Dave Giusti	PIT	1970	26		ATL	1978	25
Rawly Eastwick	CIN	1976	26		ATL	1979	25
Rich Gossage	PIT	1977	26				

Most Saves, Career

Player	SV	Player	SV
Rollie Fingers	244	Jim Brewer	132
Sparky Lyle	233	John Hiller	125
Hoyt Wilhelm	227	Jack Aker	123
Roy Face	193	Dick Radatz	122
Mike Marshall	188	Gene Garber	117
Ron Perranoski	179	Frank Linzy	111
Lindy McDaniel	172	Al Worthington	110
Tug McGraw	165	Fred Gladding	109
Stu Miller	154	Wayne Granger	108
Don McMahon	153	Ron Kline	108
Ted Abernathy	148	Johnny Murphy	107
Dave Giusti	145	Kent Tekulve	104
Clay Carroll	143	John Wyatt	103
Darold Knowles	143	Ellis Kinder	102
Dave LaRoche	141	Firpo Marberry	101
Rich Gossage	134	Terry Forster	100
Bruce Sutter	133		

An earned run is charged against a pitcher every time a runner scores without the aid of an error, a passed ball, or catcher's interference (when a catcher tips the hitter's bat with his glove). The ERA tells how many earned runs a pitcher gives up for every nine innings pitched.

An ERA under 3.00 is excellent; an ERA under 2.00 is phenomenal. Almost 90 percent of the ERAs under 2.00 were posted between 1900 and 1920, when pitchers dominated the game. That's what makes Bob Gibson's 1.12 ERA in 1968 so incredible. The brilliant Cardinal right-hander hurled 13 shutouts among his 22 victories, struck out 268 batters in 304 innings, and walked just 62.

Only two pitchers have lifetime ERAs under 2.00. Big Ed Walsh leads with 1.82, followed by Addie Joss with 1.88.

Lowest ERA Season, AL

Player	Team		ERA	Player	Team		ERA
Dutch Leonard	BOS	1914	1.01	Ed Walsh	CHI	1910	1.27
Walter Johnson	WAS	1913	1.09	Walter Johnson	WAS	1918	1.27
Addie Joss	CLE	1908	1.16	Jack Coombs	PHI	1910	1.30
Cy Young	BOS	1908	1.26				

Lowest ERA, Season, NL

Player	Team		ERA	Player	Team		ERA
Three Finger Brown	CHI	1906	1.04	Carl Lundgren	CHI	1907	1.17
Bob Gibson	STL	1968	1.12	Grover Alexander	PHI	1915	1.22
Christy Mathewson	NY	1908	1.14	Christy Mathewson	NY	1905	1.27
Jack Pfiester	CHI	1907	1.15	Three Finger Brown	CHI	1909	1.30

Bob Gibson became the first NL pitcher since 1915 to post an ERA below 1.50 with his astounding 1.12 ERA in 1968.

Baseball fans have always recognized the Triple Crown of batting: leading the league in home runs, runs batted in, and batting average. Having given the batters their due, it seems only right to recognize a similar Triple Crown for pitchers.

The three parts of the Triple Crown of pitching are most wins, lowest ERA, and most strikeouts. There have been 23 Triple Crown seasons since 1901, and they were turned in by just 13 pitchers. It's a very select group. Since 1945, only Sandy Koufax and Steve Carlton have qualified. This Triple Crown provides an important way of determining who the very best pitchers are.

Triple-Crown Pitchers, AL (most wins, lowest ERA, most strikeouts)

Player	Team		W	L	SO	ERA
Cy Young	BOS	1901	33	10	158	1.62
Walter Johnson	WAS	1913	36	7	303	1.13
	WAS	1918	23	13	162	1.27
	WAS	1924	23	7	158	2.72
Lefty Grove	PHI	1930	28	5	209	2.54
	PHI	1931	31	4	175	2.06
Lefty Gomez	NY	1934	26	5	158	2.33
	NY	1937	21	11	194	2.33
Bob Feller	CLE	1940	27	11	261	2.62
Hal Newhouser	DET	1945	25	9	212	1.81

Triple-Crown Pitchers, NL (most wins, lowest ERA, most strikeouts)

Player	Team		W	L	SO	ERA
Christy Mathewson	NY	1905	31	8	206	1.27
	NY	1908	37	11	259	1.43
Grover Alexander	PHI	1915	31	10	241	1.22
	PHI	1916	33	12	167	1.55
	PHI	1917	30	13	200	1.83
Hippo Vaughn	CHI	1918	22	10	148	1.74
Grover Alexander	CHI	1920	27	14	173	1.91
Dazzy Vance	BKN	1924	28	6	262	2.16
Bucky Walters	CIN	1939	27	11	137	2.29
Sandy Koufax	LA	1963	25	5	306	1.88
	LA	1965	26	8	382	2.04
	LA	1966	27	9	317	1.73
Steve Carlton	PHI	1972	27	10	310	1.98

PITCHING RECORDS

Won 20 and Hit .300 in Same Year, AL

Player	Team		W	L	AB	H	HR	RBI	BA
Clark Griffith	CHI	1901	24	7	89	27	2	14	.303
Cy Young	BOS	1903	28	9	137	44	1	14	.321
Ed Killian	DET	1907	25	13	122	39	0	11	.320
Jack Coombs	PHI	1911	28	12	141	45	2	23	.319
Babe Ruth	BOS	1917	24	13	123	40	2	12	.325
Carl Mays	NY	1921	27	9	143	49	2	22	.343
Joe Bush	NY	1922	26	7	95	31	0	12	.311
George Uhle	CLE	1923	26	16	144	52	0	22	.361
Joe Shaute	CLE	1924	20	17	107	34	1	10	.318
Walter Johnson	WAS	1925	20	7	97	42	2	20	.433
Ted Lyons	CHI	1930	22	15	122	36	1	15	.311
Wes Ferrell	CLE	1931	22	12	116	37	9	30	.319
Schoolboy Rowe	DET	1934	24	8	109	33	2	22	.303
Wes Ferrell	BOS	1935	25	14	150	52	7	32	.347
Red Ruffing	NY	1939	21	7	114	35	1	20	.307
Ned Garver	STL	1951	20	12	95	29	1	9	.305
Catfish Hunter	OAK	1971	21	11	103	36	1	12	.350

Won 20 and Hit .300 in Same Year, NL

Player	Team		W	L	AB	H	HR	RBI	BA
Jesse Tannehill	PIT	1900	20	6	110	37	0	17	.336
Brickyard Kennedy	BKN	1900	20	13	123	37	0	15	.301
Claude Hendrix	PIT	1912	24	9	121	39	1	15	.322
Burleigh Grimes	BKN	1920	23	11	111	34	0	16	.306
Wilbur Cooper	PIT	1924	20	14	104	36	0	15	.346
Pete Donohue	CIN	1926	20	14	106	33	0	14	.311
Burleigh Grimes	PIT	1928	25	14	131	42	0	16	.321
Curt Davis	STL	1939	22	16	105	40	1	17	.381
Bucky Walters	CIN	1939	27	11	120	39	1	16	.325
Johnny Sain	BOS	1947	21	12	107	37	0	18	.346
Don Newcombe	BKN	1955	20	5	117	42	7	23	.359
Warren Spahn	MIL	1958	22	11	108	36	2	15	.333
Don Drysdale	LA	1965	23	12	130	39	7	19	.300
Bob Gibson	STL	1970	23	7	109	33	2	19	.303

If Babe Ruth hadn't been such a great hitter, he might have been one of the best left-handed pitchers of all time. Ruth's slugging was so powerful, however, that it forced him off the mound. He was just too strong a hitter to bat every few days. Even so, Ruth still ranks as the best-hitting pitcher in baseball.

No one thinks of Walter Johnson as a hitter, but "The Big Train" had a lot of steam at the plate, too. In 1925, when the Washington Senators won the pennant, he racked up the highest season batting average ever posted by a pitcher. He slammed out 42 hits in 97 at bats for an average of .433, with six doubles, one triple, and two home runs.

There have been many other good-hitting pitchers; some have even been used as regular pinch-hitters. But with the coming of the designated hitter, many pitchers will never come to bat, and the hitting pitcher may become just a bit of baseball history.

Best-Hitting Pitchers, Career

Player	AB	H	2B	3B	HR	RBI	BA
Babe Ruth	490	149	34	11	15	73	.304
George Uhle	1363	393	60	21	9	187	.288
Doc Crandall	573	163	23	15	8	91	.284
Red Lucas	1388	392	60	13	3	183	.282
Wes Ferrell	1128	316	55	12	38	202	.280
Al Orth	1400	389	54	28	11	165	.278
Jack Scott	678	186	31	4	5	73	.274
Don Newcombe	878	238	33	3	15	108	.271
Sloppy Thurston	648	175	38	10	5	79	.270
Red Ruffing	1932	520	97	13	36	273	.269
Carl Mays	1085	291	32	21	5	110	.268
Nixey Callahan	682	181			4		.265
Johnny Marcum	533	141	18	1	5	70	.265
George Mullin	1504	397	70	23	3	135	.264
Schoolboy Rowe	909	239	36	9	18	153	.263
Fred Hutchinson	649	171	23	3	4	83	.263
Jesse Tannehill	1093	285	55	23	5	141	.261
Joe Shaute	657	170	28	4	1	63	.259
Dutch Ruether	947	245	30	12	7	111	.259
Johnny Lush	992	252	40	11	2	94	.254
Joe Bush	1239	313	59	17	7	134	.253
Mickey McDermott	619	156	29	2	9	74	.252
Clarence Mitchell	1287	324	41	10	7	133	.252
Carl Scheib	468	117	14	6	5	59	.250

Most Home Runs, Pitcher, Career

Player	HR
Wes Ferrell	38
Bob Lemon	37
Red Ruffing	36
Jack Stivetts	35
Warren Spahn	35
Earl Wilson	35
Don Drysdale	29
Bob Caruthers	28
John Clarkson	24
Walter Johnson	24
Bob Gibson	24
Milt Pappas	20
Dizzy Trout	20

Worst-Hitting Pitchers, Career (100 or more at-bats)

Player	AB	H	BA
Ron Herbel	206	6	.029
Ed Klepfer	125	6	.048
Bill Butler	117	6	.051
Taylor Phillips	113	6	.053
Bill Trotter	109	6	.055
Don Johnson	155	9	.058
Buster Narum	118	7	.059
Luke Walker	188	11	.059
Ryne Duren	114	7	.061
Marv Breuer	157	10	.064
Rip Hagerman	123	8	.065
Dean Chance	662	44	.066
Joe Engel	104	7	.067
Bob Bowman	101	7	.069
Billy McCool	101	7	.069
Mike Kilkenny	114	8	.070
Ernie Koob	128	9	.070
Bill Greif	166	12	.072
Clem Labine	227	17	.075
Pete Burnside	132	10	.076
Dick Drago	273	21	.077
Dick Woodson	117	9	.077
Wayne Simpson	153	12	.078
Bill Hands	472	37	.078
Brent Strom	102	8	.078
Lee Stange	305	24	.079
Karl Drews	254	21	.083
Ed Rakow	206	19	.084
Wilbur Wood	322	27	.084
Roger Craig	448	38	.085
Hank Aguirre	388	33	.085

Fielding Records

Rogers Hornsby, one of the greatest hitters of all time, once remarked scornfully, "Good fielders? Heck, you can pick them by the bushel!"

But fielding ability is a hidden factor in much of what happens on a baseball diamond. A fast outfielder can turn a potential extra-base hit into an out. This is of particular importance on artificial turf, where a well-hit ball can easily skip between two outfielders. Also, many balls which are hit right at an infielder can be traced to the fielder's knowledge of where the batter is likely to hit the ball.

Great fielders often get overlooked by the men who elect players to the Hall of Fame. Outstanding infielders like Luis Aparicio, Nellie Fox, Phil Rizzuto, Pee Wee Reese, and Marty Marion are still waiting for their call from Cooperstown.

Old-timers may argue, but the statistics indicate that fielding today is better than ever. Active players are at or near the top of the fielding percentage lists at every position. The major reason for this is the improved equipment. Old-timers played with gloves that barely covered a fielder's hand. Today's gloves, with their long fingers and deep pockets, make it much easier to reach the ball and hold onto it.

Most Consecutive Errorless Games by Position, AL

Player	Pos.	G	Began	Ended
Mike Hegan	1B	178	1970	1973
Jerry Adair	2B	89	1964	1965
Don Money	3B	88	1973	1974
Ed Brinkman	SS	72	1972	1972
Al Kaline	OF	242	1970	1972
Yogi Berra	C	148	1957	1958
Paul Lindblad	P	385	1966	1974

Most Consecutive Errorless Games by Position, NL

Player	Pos.	G	Began	Ended
Frank McCormick	1B	138	1945	1946
Ken Boswell	2B	85	1970	1970
Jim Davenport	3B	97	1966	1968
Buddy Kerr	SS	68	1946	1947
Curt Flood	OF	226	1965	1966
Johnny Edwards	C	138	1970	1971
Lindy McDaniel	P	225	1964	1968

Best Double-Play Combinations, Season

Player	Team		DP
Bill Mazeroski	PIT N	1966	161
Gene Alley	PIT N	1966	128
Total			289
Jerry Priddy	DET A	1950	150
Johnny Lipon	DET A	1950	126
Total			276
Bill Mazeroski	PIT N	1962	138
Dick Groat	PIT N	1962	126
Total			264
Bobby Doerr	BOS A	1949	134
Vern Stephens	BOS A	1949	128
Total			262
Bill Mazeroski	PIT N	1961	144
Dick Groat	PIT N	1961	117
Total			261
Jerry Coleman	NY A	1950	137
Phil Rizzuto	NY A	1950	123
Total			260
Bobby Knoop	CAL A	1966	135
Jim Fregosi	CAL A	1966	126
Total			260
Hughie Critz	CIN N	1928	124
Hod Ford	CIN N	1928	128
Total			252
Johnny Temple	CIN N	1954	117
Roy McMillan	CIN N	1954	129
Total			246
Ray Mack	CLE A	1943	123
Lou Boudreau	CLE A	1943	122
Total			245
Bobby Doerr	BOS A	1950	130
Vern Stephens	BOS A	1950	115
Total			245
Bill Mazeroski	PIT N	1958	118
Dick Groat	PIT N	1958	127
Total			245
Bobby Richardson	NY A	1961	136
Tony Kubek	NY A	1961	109
Total			245
Dave Cash	PHI N	1974	141
Larry Bowa	PHI N	1974	104
Total			245
Jackie Robinson	BKN N	1951	137
Pee Wee Reese	BKN N	1951	106
Total			243
Nellie Fox	CHI A	1960	126
Luis Aparicio	CHI A	1960	117
Total			243

The triple play is the most startling play in baseball. Three outs on one swing, and it's over in a flash. Often you don't realize you've seen a triple play until after it's over and the players have run off the field.

But the rarest play of them all is the unassisted triple play. There have been only eight in the whole history of baseball. All the odds are against its happening: There must be no outs, there must be two men on base, and the ball must be hit hard, right at an infielder. And even then, the fielder has to be very lucky.

The most famous unassisted triple play was pulled off by Bill Wambsganss in the 1920 World Series between the Dodgers and Indians. With runners on first and second, the Dodgers' batter smashed a hard liner toward right field. Wambsganss, playing second for the Indians, snared the drive, stepped on second base, and tagged a very surprised runner coming down from first base. This rare feat made Wambsganss famous, but he later recalled, "The only thing anyone seems to remember is that once I made an unassisted triple play in a World Series.... You'd think I was born the day before and died the day after."

Unassisted Triple Plays

Player	Team	Date	Pos.	Opp.	Opp. Batter
Neal Ball	CLE A	Jul 19, 1909	SS	BOS	Amby McConnell
Bill Wambsganss	CLE A	Oct 10, 1920	2B	BKN	Clarence Mitchell
George Burns	BOS A	Sep 14, 1923	1B	CLE	Frank Brower
Ernie Padgett	BOS N	Oct 6, 1923	SS	PHI	Walter Holke
Glenn Wright	PIT N	May 7, 1925	SS	STL	Jim Bottomley
Jimmy Cooney	CHI N	May 30, 1927	SS	PIT	Paul Waner
Johnny Neun	DET A	May 31, 1927	1B	CLE	Homer Summa
Ron Hansen	WAS A	Jul 29, 1968	SS	CLE	Joe Azcue

Cleveland second baseman **Bill Wambsganss.**

Highest Fielding Percentage By Position, Season, AL

Player	Team		Pos.	Pct.
Stuffy McInnis	BOS	1921	1B	.999
Bobby Grich	BAL	1973	2B	.995
Don Money	MIL	1974	3B	.989
Ed Brinkman	DET	1972	SS	.990
Rocky Colavito	KC	1964	OF	1.000
Mickey Stanley	DET	1968		1.000
	DET	1970		1.000
Roy White	NY	1971		1.000
Ken Berry	CAL	1972		1.000
Carl Yastrzemski	BOS	1977		1.000
Buddy Rosar	PHI	1946	C	1.000
Lou Berberet	WAS	1957		1.000
Pete Daley	BOS	1957		1.000
Yogi Berra	NY	1958		1.000
Walter Johnson	WAS	1913	P	1.000

Highest Fielding Percentage By Position, Season, NL

Player	Team		Pos.	Pct.
Frank McCormick	PHI	1946	1B	.999
Red Schoendienst	STL	1956		
	NY	1956	2B	.993
Heinie Groh	NY	1924	3B	.983
Larry Bowa	PHI	1979	SS	.991
Danny Litwhiler	PHI	1942	OF	1.000
Tony Gonzalez	PHI	1962		1.000
Curt Flood	STL	1966		1.000
Terry Puhl	HOU	1979		1.000
Wes Westrum	NY	1950	C	.999
Randy Jones	SD	1976	P	1.000

WORLD SERIES GEMS

World Series pressure brings out the best in great fielders. Many of the most famous Series moments have featured defensive gems. The Orioles' **Brooks Robinson** demoralized the Reds in the 1970 Series with plays like this diving catch in the hole between third and short *(below)*. But the most famous catch of all was the one made by **Willie Mays** in the 1954 Series on a drive hit by Cleveland's Vic Wertz. Running at full speed toward the center field fence, Mays caught the ball over his shoulder 460 feet from home plate, robbing Wertz of a sure triple and possible home run *(right)*. In one motion Mays caught the ball, whirled, and fired it back into the infield, preventing a run from scoring.

Highest Fielding Percentage By Position, Career

Player	Pos.	Pct.	Player	Pos.	Pct.
Wes Parker	1B	.996	Roger Metzger		.976
Steve Garvey		.996	Pete Rose	OF	.992
Jim Spencer		.995	Joe Rudi		.991
Bobby Grich	2B	.984	Mickey Stanley		.991
Jerry Lumpe		.984	Bill Freehan	C	.993
Dave Cash		.983	Elston Howard		.993
Brooks Robinson	3B	.971	Sherm Lollar		.992
George Kell		.969	Woody Fryman	P	.991
Don Wert		.968	Don Mossi		.990
Larry Bowa	SS	.981	Gary Nolan		.990
Mark Belanger		.977			

Larry Bowa of the Phillies, statistically the best-fielding shortstop of all time, soars over a sliding runner to complete the double play.

Rookie
Records

The Official Major League Scoring Committee defines a rookie as a player who begins a season in the majors with fewer than 50 lifetime innings pitched or fewer than 130 lifetime at bats. The odds are tremendous against any rookies ever bettering or even approaching the current records for first-year players. Among these marks are the following targets for the rookies of today to take aim at:

- The batting average of .373 posted by George Watkins of the St. Louis Cardinals in 1930
- The 38 home runs hit by Wally Berger of the Boston Braves in 1930 and by Cincinnati's Frank Robinson in 1956
- The 145 runs batted in by Ted Williams of the Boston Red Sox in 1939
- The 223 hits produced by Lloyd Waner of the Pittsburgh Pirates in 1927
- The 28 victories registered by Grover Alexander for the Philadelphia Phillies in 1911.

A total of 13 rookies have hit 30 or more homers, and 16 have collected 200 or more hits. Twenty-nine first-year pitchers have won 20 or more games. Two rookies with particularly sparkling debuts were Tony Oliva of the Twins, who won a batting title in 1964, his rookie year, and Fred Lynn, who was both Rookie of the Year and Most Valuable Player for the Red Sox in 1975.

THE YOUNGEST PLAYER

World War II caused a severe shortage of ballplayers. The many teenagers who played during those years were in demand less for their ability on the field than for the fact that they were too young for the armed forces. Even so, Cincinnati pitcher **Joe Nuxhall** *(right)* seems to have been an unlikely major leaguer. He was exactly 15 years, 10 months, and 11 days old when he was sent in to face the Cardinals in the ninth inning. He walked the first batter, retired the next two, then walked four more in a row, uncorked a wild pitch, and gave up two singles before being taken mercifully out of the game. He had given up five runs in two-thirds of an inning, but he had hardly hurt the Cincinnati cause—they lost the game 18–0.

On April 21, 1898, Bill Duggleby, who had never appeared in a major league game, was summoned by the Phillies' manager to pinch hit for the pitcher. He came in with the bases loaded to face an experienced Giant pitcher. Duggleby took a great cut, and the ball sailed over the left field fence for a grand-slam home run.

Thus Bill Duggleby became the first player ever to homer in his first look at big league pitching. In the years since, he has been joined by 45 others, although no one else has matched Duggleby's grand slam.

Eight players not only homered in their first at bat, but did it on the first pitch ever thrown to them. They were Brant Alyea, Bert Campaneris, Clise Dudley, Eddie Morgan, Don Rose, Chuck Tanner, George Vico, and Clyde Vollmer.

Home Run in First At-Bat in Majors, AL

Player	Team	Date
Earl Averill	CLE	Apr 16, 1929
Ace Parker	PHI	Apr 30, 1937
Bill LeFebvre	BOS	Jun 10, 1938
Hack Miller	DET	Apr 23, 1944
Eddie Pellagrini	BOS	Apr 22, 1946
George Vico	DET	Apr 20, 1948
Bob Nieman	STL	Sep 14, 1951
John Kennedy	WAS	Sep 5, 1962
Buster Narum	BAL	May 3, 1963
Gates Brown	DET	Jun 19, 1963
Bert Campaneris	KC	Jul 23, 1964
Bill Roman	DET	Sep 30, 1964
Brant Alyea	WAS	Sep 12, 1965
John Miller	NY	Sep 11, 1966
Rick Renick	MIN	Jul 11, 1968
Joe Keough	OAK	Aug 7, 1968
Gene Lamont	DET	Sep 2, 1970
Don Rose	CAL	May 24, 1972
Reggie Sanders	DET	Sep 1, 1974
Dave McKay	MIN	Aug 22, 1975
Al Woods	TOR	Apr 7, 1977
Dave Machemer	CAL	Jun 21, 1978

ROOKIE RECORDS

Home Run in First At-Bat in Majors, NL

Player	Team	Date
Bill Duggleby	PHI	Apr 21, 1898
Johnny Bates	BOS	Apr 12, 1906
Clise Dudley	BKN	Apr 29, 1929
Gordon Slade	BKN	May 24, 1930
Eddie Morgan	STL	Apr 14, 1936
Ernie Koy	BKN	Apr 19, 1938
Emmett Mueller	PHI	Apr 19, 1938
Clyde Vollmer	CIN	May 31, 1942
Buddy Kerr	NY	Sep 8, 1943
Whitey Lockman	NY	Jul 5, 1945
Dan Bankhead	BKN	Aug 20, 1947
Les Layton	NY	May 21, 1948
Ed Sanicki	PHI	Sep 14, 1949
Ted Tappe	CIN	Sep 14, 1950
Hoyt Wilhelm	NY	Apr 25, 1952
Wally Moon	STL	Apr 15, 1954
Chuck Tanner	MIL	Apr 12, 1955
Bill White	NY	May 7, 1956
Frank Ernaga	CHI	May 24, 1957
Don Leppert	PIT	Jun 18, 1961
Cuno Barragan	CHI	Sep 1, 1961
Benny Ayala	NY	Aug 27, 1974
Jose Sosa	HOU	Jul 30, 1975
Johnnie LeMaster	SF	Sep 2, 1975
Tim Wallach	MON	Sep 6, 1980

Pinch-Hit Home Run in First At-Bat in Majors, AL

Player	Team	Date	Inn.
Ace Parker	PHI	Apr 30, 1937	8
John Kennedy	WAS	Sep 5, 1962	6
Gates Brown	DET	Jun 19, 1963	5
Bill Roman	DET	Sep 30, 1964	7
Brant Alyea	WAS	Sep 12, 1965	6
Joe Keough	OAK	Aug 7, 1968	8
Al Woods	TOR	Apr 7, 1977	5

Pinch-Hit Home Run in First At-Bat in Majors, NL

Player	Team	Date	Inn.
Eddie Morgan	STL	Apr 14, 1936	7
Les Layton	NY	May 21, 1948	9
Ted Tappe	CIN	Sep 14, 1950	8
Chuck Tanner	MIL	Apr 12, 1955	8

Thirty or More Home Runs, Rookie, AL

Player	Team		HR
Al Rosen	CLE	1950	37
Hal Trosky	CLE	1934	35
Rudy York	DET	1937	35
Walt Dropo	BOS	1950	34
Jimmie Hall	MIN	1963	33
Tony Oliva	MIN	1964	32
Ted Williams	BOS	1939	31
Bob Allison	WAS	1959	30

Thirty or More Home Runs, Rookie, NL

Player	Team		HR
Wally Berger	BOS	1930	38
Frank Robinson	CIN	1956	38
Earl Williams	ATL	1971	33
Jim Hart	SF	1964	31
Willie Montanez	PHI	1971	30

Frank Robinson (top) and **Wally Berger** (above) share the major league record for home runs by a rookie with 38 each. **Al Rosen** (right) set the AL mark in 1950, when he hit 37.

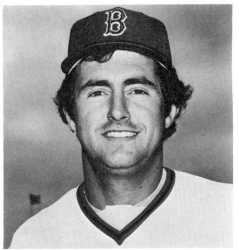

Highest Batting Average, Rookie, AL

Player	Team		BA
Dale Alexander	DET	1929	.343
Patsy Dougherty	BOS	1902	.342
Earle Combs	NY	1925	.342
Socks Seybold	PHI	1901	.334
Heinie Manush	DET	1923	.334
Charlie Keller	NY	1939	.334
Mickey Cochrane	PHI	1925	.331
Earl Averill	CLE	1929	.331
Johnny Pesky	BOS	1942	.331
Fred Lynn	BOS	1975	.331

Highest Batting Average, Rookie, NL

Player	Team		BA
George Watkins	STL	1930	.373
Jimmy Williams	PIT	1899	.355
Lloyd Waner	PIT	1927	.355
Chick Stahl	BOS	1897	.354
Kiki Cuyler	PIT	1924	.354
Fielder Jones	BKN	1896	.353
Ginger Beaumont	PIT	1899	.352
Richie Ashburn	PHI	1948	.333
Rico Carty	MIL	1964	.330
Johnny Mize	STL	1936	.329

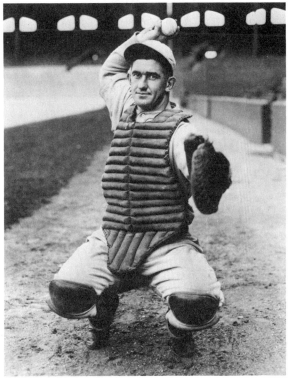

Tony Oliva *(top left)* won AL batting titles in his first two seasons. **Fred Lynn** *(top right)* is the only rookie to win the Most Valuable Player Award. **Mickey Cochrane** *(above)* followed his great rookie year with 13 seasons as one of the game's best catchers.

ROOKIE RECORDS

Shutout in First Game in Majors, AL

Player	Team	Date	Score	Inns.	Opp.
Jesse Stovall	CLE	Sep 3, 1903	1-0	11	DET
Jack Coombs	PHI	Jul 15, 1906	3-0		WAS
Slow Joe Doyle	NY	Aug 25, 1906	2-0		CLE
Rube Kroh	BOS	Sep 30, 1906	2-0		STL
Tacks Neuer	NY	Aug 28, 1907	1-0		BOS
Pete Wilson	NY	Sep 15, 1908	1-0		BOS
Larry Pape	BOS	Jul 6, 1909	2-0		WAS
Fred Blanding	CLE	Sep 15, 1910	3-0		WAS
Lefty Russell	PHI	Oct 1, 1910	3-0		BOS
Buck O'Brien	BOS	Sep 9, 1911	2-0		PHI
Stan Coveleski	PHI	Sep 12, 1912	3-0		DET
Bob Shawkey	PHI	Jul 25, 1913	4-0		DET
Marty McHale	NY	Sep 11, 1913	4-0		STL
Doc Ayers	WAS	Sep 30, 1913	3-0		PHI
Jack Bentley	WAS	Oct 1, 1913	1-0	8	PHI
George Dumont	WAS	Sep 14, 1915	3-0		CLE
Elmer Myers	PHI	Oct 6, 1915	4-0		WAS
Claude Thomas	WAS	Sep 18, 1916	1-0		PHI
Bob Clark	CLE	Aug 15, 1920	5-0		DET
Danny Boone	CLE	Aug 20, 1922	2-0	12	WAS
Russ Van Atta	NY	Apr 25, 1933	16-0		WAS
Johnny Marcum	PHI	Sep 7, 1933	6-0		CLE
Henry Coppola	WAS	Jun 6, 1935	3-0		PHI
George Gill	DET	May 12, 1937	4-0		BOS
Bill Phebus	WAS	Sep 4, 1937	1-0		BOS
Boo Ferriss	BOS	Apr 25, 1945	5-0		NY
Fred Sanford	STL	Sep 15, 1946	1-0		NY
Sandy Consuegra	WAS	Jun 10, 1950	6-0	5	CHI
Mike Fornieles	WAS	Sep 2, 1952	5-0		PHI
Bobo Holloman	STL	May 6, 1953	6-0		PHI
Ben Flowers	BOS	Aug 5, 1953	5-0		STL
Lew Krausse	KC	Jun 16, 1961	4-0		LA
Dave McNally	BAL	Sep 26, 1962	3-0		KC
Tom Phoebus	BAL	Sep 15, 1966	2-0		CAL
Billy Rohr	BOS	Apr 14, 1967	3-0		NY
Mike Norris	OAK	Apr 10, 1975	9-0		CHI

Shutout in First Game in Majors, NL

Player	Team	Date	Score	Inns.	Opp.
Alex Hardy	CHI	Sep 4, 1902	1-0		BKN
Red Ames	NY	Sep 14, 1903	5-0	5	STL
Lefty Leifield	PIT	Sep 3, 1905	1-0	6	CHI
Vive Lindaman	BOS	Apr 14, 1906	1-0		BKN
Howie Camnitz	PIT	Sep 28, 1906	1-0	7	BKN
Nick Maddox	PIT	Sep 13, 1907	4-0		STL
George McQuillan	PHI	Sep 22, 1907	2-0	6	STL
Bob Spade	CIN	Sep 22, 1907	1-0		NY
Tom Tuckey	BOS	Aug 11, 1908	2-0		STL
Cliff Curtis	BOS	Sep 2, 1909	1-0		PIT
Eddie Stack	PHI	Jun 7, 1910	1-0		CHI
Wilbur Cooper	PIT	Sep 6, 1912	8-0		STL
Pete Schneider	CIN	Jun 28, 1914	1-0		PIT
Carmen Hill	PIT	Apr 17, 1915	5-0		NY
Vic Aldridge	CHI	May 16, 1917	8-0		BOS
Harry Shriver	BKN	May 1, 1922	2-0		PHI
Tim McNamara	BOS	Sep 27, 1922	7-0		BKN
Earl Caldwell	PHI	Sep 8, 1928	5-0	6	BOS
Van Mungo	BKN	Sep 7, 1931	2-0		BOS
Ray Starr	STL	Sep 15, 1932	3-0		BKN
Hal Smith	PIT	Sep 22, 1932	7-0		CHI
Bill Lee	CHI	May 7, 1934	2-0		PHI
Oad Swigart	PIT	Sep 21, 1939	7-0		BOS
Don Newcombe	BKN	May 22, 1949	3-0		CIN
Bill Macdonald	PIT	May 23, 1950	6-0		PHI
Paul LaPalme	PIT	Jun 5, 1951	8-0		BOS
Niles Jordan	PHI	Aug 26, 1951	8-0		CIN
Jackie Collum	STL	Sep 21, 1951	6-0		CHI
Stu Miller	STL	Aug 15, 1952	1-0	6	CHI
Al Worthington	NY	Jul 6, 1953	6-0		PIT
Karl Spooner	BKN	Sep 22, 1954	3-0		NY
Von McDaniel	STL	Jun 21, 1957	2-0		BKN
Carl Willey	MIL	Jun 23, 1958	7-0		SF
Nick Willhite	LA	Jun 11, 1963	2-0		CHI
Grover Powell	NY	Aug 20, 1963	4-0		PHI
Dick Rusteck	NY	Jun 10, 1966	5-0		CIN
Wayne Simpson	CIN	Apr 9, 1970	3-0		LA
Ed Acosta	SD	Aug 24, 1971	2-0		PHI
Dave Downs	PHI	Sep 2, 1972	3-0		ATL
Eric Rasmussen	STL	Jul 21, 1975	4-0		SD
Charlie Leibrandt	CIN	Apr 13, 1980	5-0		ATL
Marty Bystrom	PHI	Sep 10, 1980	5-0		NY

Twenty or More Wins, Rookie, AL

Player	Team		W	L	Player	Team		W	L
Russ Ford	NY	1910	26	6	Reb Russell	CHI	1913	21	17
Ed Summers	DET	1908	24	8	Scott Perry	PHI	1918	21	19
Vean Gregg	CLE	1911	23	7	Bob Grim	NY	1954	20	6
Roscoe Miller	DET	1901	23	13	Gene Bearden	CLE	1948	20	7
Monte Weaver	WAS	1932	22	10	Hugh Bedient	BOS	1912	20	10
Wes Ferrell	CLE	1929	21	10	Alex Kellner	PHI	1949	20	12
Boo Ferriss	BOS	1945	21	10	Roy Patterson	CHI	1901	20	16

Twenty or More Wins, Rookie, NL

Player	Team		W	L	Player	Team		W	L
Grover Alexander	PHI	1911	28	13	Jack Pfiester	CHI	1906	20	8
Larry Cheney	CHI	1912	26	10	Jake Weimer	CHI	1903	20	8
Jeff Pfeffer	BKN	1914	23	12	Cliff Melton	NY	1937	20	9
George McQuillan	PHI	1908	23	17	Harvey Haddix	STL	1953	20	9
Larry Jansen	NY	1947	21	5	Lou Fette	BOS	1937	20	10
Johnny Beazley	STL	1942	21	6	Jim Turner	BOS	1937	20	11
Henry Schmidt	BKN	1903	21	13	Christy Mathewson	NY	1901	20	17
Bill Voiselle	NY	1944	21	16	Irv Young	BOS	1905	20	21
King Cole	CHI	1910	20	4					

Rookie No-Hitters, AL

Player	Team	Date	Score	Opp.
Charlie Robertson	CHI	Apr 30, 1922	2-0	DET
Vern Kennedy	CHI	Aug 31, 1935	5-0	CLE
Bill McCahan	PHI	Sep 3, 1947	3-0	WAS
Bobo Holloman	STL	May 6, 1953	6-0	PHI
Bo Belinsky	LA	May 5, 1962	2-0	BAL
Vida Blue	OAK	Sep 21, 1970	6-0	MIN
Steve Busby	KC	Apr 27, 1973	3-0	DET

Rookie No-Hitters, NL

Player	Team	Date	Score	Opp.
Larry Corcoran	CHI	Aug 19, 1880	6-0	BOS
Bumpus Jones	CIN	Oct 15, 1892	7-1	PIT
Jim Hughes	BAL	Apr 22, 1898	8-0	BOS
Deacon Phillippe	LOU	May 25, 1899	7-0	NY
Nick Maddox	PIT	Sep 20, 1907	2-1	BKN
Jeff Tesreau	NY	Sep 6, 1912	3-0	PHI
Paul Dean	STL	Sep 21, 1934	3-0	BKN
Burt Hooton	CHI	Apr 16, 1972	4-0	NY

TEENAGED BALLPLAYERS

Major league teams are no longer allowed to sign high-school players until they have graduated, so Joe Nuxhall's distinction as the youngest player in major league history appears secure. Nuxhall made his debut with Cincinnati in 1944 when he was just 15 years old.

Tommy Brown of the Dodgers was the youngest player ever to hit a home run when he smashed one on August 20, 1945. He was four months shy of his eighteenth birthday. Tony Conigliaro is the only teenager to lead his league in home runs, hitting 32 for the 1965 Red Sox when he was 19. While no teenaged pitcher in this century has won 20 games in a season, one, Wally Bunker of the Orioles, fell just short, winning 19 in 1964 at age 19. Current ballplayers who broke into the big leagues as teenagers include Robin Yount, Jack Clark, Alfredo Griffin, John Mayberry, Willie Montanez, Bert Blyleven, and Rowland Office.

Major Leaguers Under 18

AMERICAN LEAGUE				Age	NATIONAL LEAGUE		
Player	Team	First Year			Player	Team	First Year
				15	Joe Nuxhall	CIN	1944
Carl Scheib	PHI	1943		16	Tommy Brown	BKN	1944
Alex George	KC	1955					
Jim Derrington	CHI	1956					
Owen Shannon	STL	1903		17	Mike Loan	PHI	1912
Dave Skeels	DET	1910			Mel Ott	NY	1926
Bob Williams	NY	1911			Putsy Caballero	PHI	1944
Merito Acosta	WAS	1913			Granny Hamner	PHI	1944
Charlie Grimm	PHI	1916			Erv Palica	BKN	1945
Jimmie Foxx	PHI	1925			Harry Chiti	CHI	1950
Bob Feller	CLE	1936			Rod Miller	BKN	1957
Vern Frieberger	CLE	1941			Tim McCarver	STL	1959
Bob G. Miller	DET	1953			Danny Murphy	CHI	1960
Harmon Killebrew	WAS	1954			Ed Kranepool	NY	1962
					Jay Dahl	HOU	1963

ROOKIE RECORDS

Most Wins by Age, AL

Player	Team			Age	W
Bob Feller	CLE	1936		17	5
	CLE	1937		18	9
Wally Bunker	BAL	1964		19	19
Bob Feller	CLE	1939		20	20
	CLE	1940		21	27

Most Wins by Age, NL

Player	Team			Age	W
Mike McCormick	SF	1957		18	3
Gary Nolan	CIN	1967		19	14
Christy Mathewson	NY	1901		20	20
Rube Marquard	NY	1911		21	24

Few pitchers have been as good as young as **Bob Feller.** "Rapid Robert," the fireballer from Van Meter, Iowa, won a total of 55 games before his 21st birthday.

Expansion:
1960-1969

Events in the outside world caused major changes in baseball during the 1940s and 1950s, but the changes of the 1960s were baseball's own doing. Baseball owners had to face up to the rising popularity of football and fight charges that baseball was too dull and old-fashioned. One measure of the changes in the game is the fact that the 1969 World Series was won by a team that didn't even exist until 1962.

Thanks to television, fans in cities that did not have teams could follow baseball in the 1960s, and this led to a demand for teams in more cities. Thus, two teams were added to the American League in 1961—Los Angeles (soon to move down to Anaheim as the California Angels) and Washington (to replace the old Senators, who had become the Minnesota Twins). The next year, the National League added teams in New York and Houston. The New York Mets quickly proved themselves the worst team in baseball history by losing a record 120 games. The Houston Colt .45s would soon become the Astros and move into the world's first indoor stadium, the Astrodome.

With the addition of all the new teams, talent was spread thinner, and the regular season was extended from 154 to 162 games. This combination made some drop-off in the quality of play inevitable, especially in pitching. This led to the first major assault on Babe Ruth's magic 60 home-run mark in more than 20 years. Mickey Mantle began the 1961 season in a blaze of home runs, then fell off the pace to end with 54. But his Yankee teammate Roger Maris just kept going and in the last game of the year hit his sixty-first home run of the season off Tracy Stallard of the Red Sox.

The Yankees ran off five straight pennants but lost three of the five Series. The once proud dynasty then crumbled, falling to a sixth place finish in 1965, and tenth the next year. The Dodgers and Cardinals stepped in, each appearing in three Series and winning two. Both were led by dominant fastball pitchers—Sandy Koufax for the Dodgers and Bob Gibson for the Cards. Koufax led the National League in wins, earned-run average, strikeouts, and shutouts in each of the Dodgers' pennant-winning years. Gibson's ERA of 1.12 in 1968 was the lowest in the majors since 1914 and capped a season in which the pitchers had clearly gained the upper hand. Detroit's Denny McLain became the first 30-game winner since Dizzy Dean, and Carl Yastrzemski led the American League with a .301 batting average, the lowest ever to lead a league.

The two leagues expanded again in 1969. The San Diego Padres joined the National League, along with the first franchise ever outside the United States, the Montreal Expos. The American League added a new team in Kansas City, the Royals, to replace the Athletics, who had moved on to Oakland. The other new AL team was the Seattle Pilots, who would stay one year before becoming the Milwaukee Brewers, filling a gap left when the Braves moved to Atlanta.

The two leagues each split into two six-team divisions, creating a play-off between the divisional winners to determine the league champion. The first club to emerge from this system was the surprising New York Mets, led by the pitching of Tom Seaver, Jerry Koosman, and Tug McGraw, who upset the Baltimore Orioles in a five-game Series to become the most unlikely champions ever.

THE YEAR OF THE PITCHER

In 1968 the pitchers took control of the game. Bob Gibson *(right)* had an amazing ERA of 1.12, and Don Drysdale *(below left)* set a record by pitching 58⅔ consecutive shutout innings. In the American League, Denny McLain *(below right)* was the first 30-game winner since the 1930s, posting a record of 31–6. The American League as a whole batted just .230; Oakland led with a team batting average of .240. The rules-makers responded by lowering the pitching mound and shrinking the strike zone. The next year, batting averages went up 7 points in the National League and 10 points in the American League.

THE DOME

Baseball entered the space age with the opening of the Houston Astrodome in 1965. The first indoor stadium posed new problems for players and groundskeepers. The glare of the sun on the roof made it hard for outfielders to see fly balls, so the roof was painted to reduce the glare. This killed the grass on the field. The next year the field was replaced by a new surface called Astroturf. This artificial turf requires less care than a grass field and is now used by 10 of the 26 major league teams.

WILLIE MAYS

Willie Mays burst into the majors in 1951, winning the Rookie of the Year Award for his electrifying play in centerfield. The Giants won the pennant that year and fielded the first all-black outfield in the major leagues—Monte Irvin, Mays, and Hank Thompson *(top, left to right)*. Mays could hit, slug, run, throw, and field with an athletic grace all his own. He combined speed and power in a manner never before seen. He flew across the outfield, reaching most balls in time to make his patented basket catch. In his 22-year career, he never ceased to show his delight in the game he played and the way he played it.

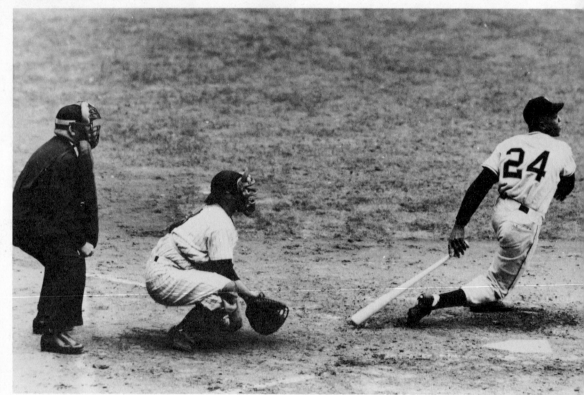

SANDY KOUFAX

Sandy Koufax played for twelve years with the Dodgers but spent the first six trying to control his blazing fastball. Once he did, he became the best pitcher in baseball and perhaps the best lefthander in history. Koufax led the National League in ERA each year from 1962 to 1966 despite an elbow so sore he had to soak it in ice for hours after every game. The strain on his arm forced him into retirement after the 1966 season, when he was just 30 years old.

HANK AARON

It would be difficult to imagine a less likely successor to Babe Ruth as baseball's home run king than Hank Aaron. Aaron was virtually unnoticed by the public during much of his career, winning just two batting titles and four home-run crowns in his 23 years in the majors. He went quietly about his business, hitting home runs and frightening opposing pitchers but never attracting the attention given to more colorful players. Like Joe DiMaggio, he was excellent without being spectacular, but his endurance and consistency made him the top home-run hitter of all time.

Team
Records

In 1950, the Associated Press conducted a poll of the nation's top sportswriters and sportscasters to select the greatest baseball team of all time. The 1927 Yankees were easy winners.

The Yankees finished 19 games ahead of the second-place Philadelphia Athletics that year. "We had a great team," recalled Al Simmons, the star outfielder for the world champion Athletics of 1929 and 1930. "But when you compare us with the really great Yankee world champions who preceded us, we simply weren't in their class. I'm not trying to kid myself nor anyone else. I fought those Yankees as hard as anyone in the American League, but when they got us into a tough series, they just batted our brains out."

Babe Ruth anchored the outfield, hitting .356 with 60 home runs. The other regular outfielders were Earle Combs, who also hit .356 and led the league with 231 hits, and Bob Meusel, a .337 hitter for the season. The infield featured Lou Gehrig at first (.373, 47 homers), Tony Lazzeri at second (.309, 102 RBIs), Mark Koenig at short (.285), and Joe Dugan at third. The catchers were Pat Collins and Johnny Grabowski, and the pitching staff included future Hall of Famers Herb Pennock and Waite Hoyt. Ruth, Gehrig, Meusel, and Lazzeri formed the heart of the batting order, and each finished the season with more than 100 RBIs.

Other teams have won more games, have had a higher team batting average, and have won the pennant by a wider margin. But no team has ever combined power, pitching, and fielding skill like the 1927 Yankees.

Greatest Teams

Manager	Team		W	L	BA	FA	ERA
Miller Huggins	NY A	1927	110	48	.309	.969	3.20
Connie Mack	PHI A	1931	107	45	.287	.975	3.47
Earl Weaver	BAL A	1970	108	54	.257	.981	3.15
Ralph Houk	NY A	1961	109	53	.263	.980	3.46
Billy Southworth	STL N	1942	106	48	.268	.972	2.55
Sparky Anderson	CIN N	1975	108	54	.271	.984	2.92
Frank Chance	CHI N	1906	116	36	.262	.969	1.76
Fred Clarke	PIT N	1909	110	42	.260	.964	2.07
Joe McCarthy	NY A	1936	102	51	.300	.973	4.17
John McGraw	NY N	1921	94	59	.298	.970	3.55
Kid Gleason	CHI A	1919	88	52	.287	.969	3.04
Walter Alston	BKN N	1955	98	55	.271	.977	3.68
Al Lopez	CLE A	1954	111	43	.262	.978	2.78
Casey Stengel	NY A	1953	99	52	.273	.978	3.20
Dick Williams	OAK A	1973	94	68	.260	.978	3.29
Fred Haney	MIL N	1957	95	59	.269	.980	3.47
Red Schoendienst	STL N	1967	101	60	.263	.977	3.05
Walter Alston	LA N	1963	99	63	.251	.975	2.98
Connie Mack	PHI A	1911	101	50	.296	.964	3.01
John McGraw	NY N	1924	90	60	.300	.971	3.62
Joe Cronin	BOS A	1946	104	50	.271	.977	3.38
Jake Stahl	BOS A	1912	105	47	.270	.957	2.76
Tris Speaker	CLE A	1920	94	60	.308	.967	3.90
Casey Stengel	NY A	1950	98	56	.282	.980	4.85
Frankie Frisch	STL N	1934	95	58	.288	.972	3.69

Who is the best manager in baseball history? In a poll of sportswriters taken in 1969, Casey Stengel edged out John McGraw for top honors. There are those who insist Joe McCarthy was the greatest, while others give the nod to Connie Mack. Present day fans can't imagine anyone was ever better than Earl Weaver, though Billy Martin has had remarkable success with five different teams. Can the records help us?

Connie Mack won the most games—3,776—but he also managed for the most years— 53. Mack never had to worry about losing his job, since he also owned the team. John McGraw and Casey Stengel managed the most pennant-winners—10—but McGraw managed for 33 years, and Stengel lasted for 25.

One possible measure is the lifetime won-lost percentage for managers with 1,000 or more wins. McCarthy, who managed the Cubs and Yankees to nine titles, leads this category. His won-lost percentage was .614. Earl Weaver is a surprising second, with a percentage of .599. His teams have never finished lower than fourth.

The best manager? Well, it's hard to say from these statistics, but they all point to the conclusion that the best manager is the man who manages the best players.

Most League Pennants Won, Manager

Manager	Total	Manager	Total
Casey Stengel	10	Miller Huggins	6
John McGraw	10	Cap Anson	5
Connie Mack	9	Frank Selee	5
Joe McCarthy	9	Ned Hanlon	5
Walter Alston	7		

Casey Stengel, Yankee manager and marathon talker, directing his defense.

Connie Mack and **John McGraw** *(far left, left to right)* represent 86 years of managing and over 6,000 wins. **Earl Weaver's** tenure with the Orioles is the longest among active managers *(right)*.

Most Wins, Manager, Career

Manager	Yrs.	W	L	Pct.	Manager	Yrs.	W	L	Pct.
Connie Mack	53	3776	4025	.484	Frank Selee	12	1299	872	.598
John McGraw	33	2824	1984	.589	Cap Anson	20	1297	957	.575
Bucky Harris	29	2159	2219	.493	Charlie Grimm	19	1287	1069	.546
Joe McCarthy	24	2126	1335	.614	Billy Rigney	17	1239	1321	.484
Walter Alston	23	2040	1613	.556	Joe Cronin	15	1236	1055	.540
Leo Durocher	24	2010	1710	.540	Earl Weaver	13	1201	805	.599
Casey Stengel	25	1926	1867	.508	Lou Boudreau	16	1162	1224	.487
Bill McKechnie	25	1898	1724	.524	Frankie Frisch	16	1137	1078	.513
Fred Clarke	19	1602	1179	.576	Hughie Jennings	14	1131	972	.538
Gene Mauch	21	1524	1705	.471	Danny Murtaugh	15	1115	950	.540
Clark Griffith	20	1491	1367	.522	Billy Southworth	13	1064	729	.593
Jimmy Dykes	31	1407	1538	.478	Steve O'Neill	18	1042	848	.551
Al Lopez	16	1414	1017	.582	Harry Wright	14	1039	819	.559
Miller Huggins	17	1413	1134	.555	Chuck Dressen	13	1031	911	.531
Wilbert Robinson	19	1397	1395	.500	Dick Williams	13	1017	944	.520
Ned Hanlon	19	1315	1167	.530	Red Schoendienst	12	1003	749	.572
Ralph Houk	16	1307	1249	.511	Sparky Anderson	11	1003	714	.584

TEAM RECORDS

Most Wins, Season, AL

Team		W	L	Pct.	Place
CLE	1954	111	43	.721	1
NY	1927	110	44	.714	1
NY	1961	109	53	.673	1
BAL	1969	109	53	.673	1
BAL	1970	108	54	.667	1
PHI	1931	107	45	.704	1
NY	1932	107	47	.695	1
NY	1939	106	45	.702	1
BOS	1912	105	47	.691	1
PHI	1929	104	46	.693	1
BOS	1946	104	50	.675	1
NY	1963	104	57	.646	1
NY	1942	103	51	.669	1
NY	1954	103	51	.669	2
DET	1968	103	59	.636	1
NY	1980	103	59	.636	1
PHI	1910	102	48	.680	1
PHI	1930	102	52	.662	1
NY	1936	102	51	.667	1
NY	1937	102	52	.662	1
MIN	1965	102	60	.630	1
KC	1977	102	60	.630	1
BAL	1979	102	57	.642	1
PHI	1911	101	50	.669	1
BOS	1915	101	50	.669	1
NY	1928	101	53	.656	1
DET	1934	101	53	.656	1
NY	1941	101	53	.656	1
DET	1961	101	61	.623	2
BAL	1971	101	57	.639	1
OAK	1971	101	60	.627	1
DET	1915	100	54	.649	2
CHI	1917	100	54	.649	1
NY	1977	100	62	.617	1
NY	1978	100	63	.613	1
BAL	1980	100	62	.617	2

No team has ever won as many games as the Chicago Cubs of 1906. Led by manager/first baseman Frank Chance, the Cubs won 116 games, losing just 36, and finished 20 games ahead of the second-place Giants. This Cubs team is considered one of the greatest of all time, even though they were upset in the World Series by their cross-town rivals, the White Sox. Known as the "Hitless Wonders," the White Sox won the AL pennant despite a team batting average of .230. They hit just six home runs all year, but became world champions thanks to their strong pitching staff, led by the great spitballer Ed Walsh.

The American League's most successful team, the 1954 Cleveland Indians, was also beaten in the World Series after winning 111 games during the regular season. The Indians were wiped out in four straight games by the Giants, led by the pinch-hitting heroics of James Lamar "Dusty" Rhodes. Rhodes won the first game with a tenth-inning pinch home run, tied the second game with a pinch single, later adding an insurance run with another homer, and drove in what proved to be the winning run with yet another pinch single in the third game. Not bad for a part-time outfielder with a lifetime batting average of .253!

Most Wins, Season, NL

Team		W	L	Pct.	Place
CHI	1906	116	36	.763	1
PIT	1909	110	42	.724	1
CIN	1975	108	54	.667	1
CHI	1907	107	45	.704	1
NY	1904	106	47	.693	1
STL	1942	106	48	.688	1
NY	1905	105	48	.686	1
STL	1942	105	49	.682	1
STL	1943	105	49	.682	1
BKN	1953	105	49	.682	1
CHI	1909	104	49	.680	2
CHI	1910	104	50	.675	1
BKN	1942	104	50	.675	2
PIT	1902	103	36	.741	1
NY	1912	103	48	.682	1
SF	1962	103	62	.624	1
LA	1962	102	63	.618	2
CIN	1970	102	60	.630	1
LA	1974	102	60	.630	1
CIN	1976	102	60	.630	1
NY	1913	101	51	.664	1
STL	1931	101	53	.656	1
STL	1967	101	60	.627	1
PHI	1976	101	61	.623	1
PHI	1977	101	61	.623	1
CHI	1935	100	54	.649	1
CIN	1940	100	53	.654	1
BKN	1941	100	54	.649	1
NY	1969	100	62	.617	1

TEAM RECORDS

Most Losses, Season, AL

Team		W	L	Pct.	Place
PHI	1916	36	117	.235	8
WAS	1904	38	113	.251	8
BOS	1932	43	111	.279	8
STL	1939	43	111	.279	8
WAS	1909	42	110	.276	8
PHI	1915	47	109	.283	8
TOR	1979	53	109	.327	7
STL	1937	46	108	.299	8
OAK	1979	54	108	.333	7
BOS	1926	46	107	.301	8
TOR	1977	54	107	.335	7
PHI	1920	48	106	.312	8
WAS	1963	56	106	.346	10
CHI	1970	56	106	.346	6
BOS	1906	49	105	.318	8
BOS	1925	47	105	.309	8
PHI	1943	49	105	.318	8
PHI	1946	49	105	.318	8
KC	1964	57	105	.352	10
PHI	1919	36	104	.257	8
WAS	1949	50	104	.325	8
DET	1952	50	104	.325	8
SEA	1978	58	104	.350	7
NY	1908	51	103	.331	8
BOS	1927	51	103	.331	8
PHI	1954	51	103	.331	8
KC	1965	59	103	.364	10
SEA	1980	59	103	.364	7
WAS	1907	49	102	.325	8
NY	1912	50	102	.329	8
BOS	1930	52	102	.338	8
CHI	1932	49	102	.325	7
PHI	1950	52	102	.338	8
STL	1951	52	102	.338	8
KC	1956	52	102	.338	8
CLE	1971	60	102	.370	6
DET	1975	57	102	.358	6
TOR	1978	59	102	.366	7
STL	1912	53	101	.344	7
CHI	1948	51	101	.336	8
STL	1949	53	101	.344	7
WAS	1955	53	101	.344	8
WAS	1962	60	101	.373	10

TEAM RECORDS

Most Losses, Season, NL

Team		W	L	Pct.	Place
NY	1962	40	120	.250	10
BOS	1935	38	115	.248	8
PIT	1952	42	112	.273	8
NY	1965	50	112	.309	10
PHI	1941	43	111	.279	8
NY	1963	51	111	.315	10
MON	1969	52	110	.321	6
SD	1969	52	110	.321	6
PHI	1928	43	109	.283	8
PHI	1942	42	109	.278	8
NY	1964	53	109	.327	10
BOS	1909	45	108	.294	8
PHI	1945	46	108	.299	8
BOS	1911	44	107	.291	8
PHI	1961	47	107	.305	8
MON	1976	55	107	.340	6
PHI	1939	45	106	.298	8
STL	1908	49	105	.318	8
PHI	1938	45	105	.300	8
BKN	1905	48	104	.316	8
PHI	1923	50	104	.325	8
PIT	1953	50	104	.325	8
BOS	1905	51	103	331	7
PIT	1917	51	103	.331	8
PHI	1921	51	103	.331	8
PHI	1927	51	103	.331	8
BOS	1928	50	103	.327	7
PHI	1940	50	103	.327	8
CHI	1962	59	103	.364	9
CHI	1966	59	103	.364	10
BOS	1906	49	102	.375	8
PHI	1930	52	102	.338	8
SD	1973	60	102	.370	6
SD	1974	60	102	.370	6
STL	1907	52	101	.340	8
BKN	1908	53	101	.344	7
BOS	1912	52	101	.340	8
PIT	1954	53	101	.344	8
NY	1967	61	101	.377	10
ATL	1977	61	101	.377	6

The most lopsided shutout in major league history came on August 21, 1883. Providence, behind Hoss Radbourn, defeated Philadelphia by a score of 28–0. The highest shutout score since 1900 was the 22–0 pasting inflicted on the Chicago Cubs by the Pittsburgh Pirates on September 16, 1975. The Pirates led 18–0 after just 4½ innings. This was the game in which Rennie Stennett, the Pirates' second baseman, became just the second major leaguer to get seven hits in a nine-inning ballgame.

Most Lopsided Wins (since 1900)

Team	Date	Loser	Score	Diff.
BOS A	Jun 8, 1950	STL	29-4	25
CLE A	Jul 7, 1923	BOS	27-3	24
CIN N	Jun 4, 1911	BOS	26-3	23
NY A	May 24, 1936	PHI	25-2	23
CHI A	Apr 23, 1955	KC	29-6	23
PHI A	May 18, 1912	DET	24-2	22
STL N	Jul 6, 1929	PHI	28-6	22
PIT N	Sep 16, 1975	CHI	22-0	22
CAL A	Aug 25, 1979	TOR	24-2	22
DET A	Sep 15, 1901	CLE	21-0	21
NY A	Aug 13, 1939	PHI	21-0	21
BOS A	Sep 27, 1940	WAS	24-4	20
BKN N	Sep 23, 1901	CIN	25-6	19
CHI N	Jun 7, 1906	NY	19-0	19
DET A	Jul 17, 1908	PHI	21-2	19
BOS N	Sep 18, 1915	STL	20-1	19
CIN N	Jul 6, 1949	CHI	23-4	19
BOS A	Apr 30, 1950	PHI	19-0	19
CLE A	May 18, 1955	BOS	19-0	19
CHI N	May 13, 1969	NY	19-0	19
LA N	Jun 28, 1969	SD	19-0	19
MON N	Jul 30, 1978	ATL	19-0	19
NY A	Jul 14, 1904	CLE	21-3	18
BKN N	Sep 3, 1906	PHI	18-0	18
PHI N	Jul 11, 1910	PIT	18-0	18
PHI A	Jul 25, 1921	CLE	21-3	18
DET A	Jun 17, 1925	NY	19-1	18
PIT N	Jun 22, 1925	STL	24-6	18
CLE A	Jul 29, 1928	NY	24-6	18
PHI A	May 1, 1929	BOS	24-6	18
CLE A	May 11, 1930	PHI	25-7	18
PHI N	Aug 10, 1930	CIN	18-0	18
STL N	Jun 10, 1934	CIN	18-0	18
PHI N	Jul 14, 1934	CIN	18-0	18
DET A	Apr 29, 1935	STL	18-0	18
NY N	Apr 30, 1944	BKN	26-8	18
KC A	Apr 25, 1961	MIN	20-2	18
CIN N	Aug 8, 1965	LA	18-0	18
CAL A	Jun 20, 1980	BOS	20-2	18

Fans love Chicago's Wrigley Field. Its short fences and ivy-covered walls give it a special charm and make spectators feel as if they're right on top of the field. For the same reason, pitchers hate Wrigley Field. The short fences make home runs out of many fly balls that would be outs in other parks. No wonder, then, that the NL home-run record is held by a Cub, Hack Wilson, who hit 56 in 1930.

No wonder, also, that the two highest-scoring games in major league history were both played in the "friendly confines" of Wrigley Field. On August 25, 1922, the Cubs leaped to a 25–6 lead and then held on to defeat the Phillies 26–23 for a record total of 49 runs. Fifty-seven years later, the same two teams played a ten-inning 23–22 game, decided by Mike Schmidt's tenth-inning home run.

Most Runs, Game, AL

Team	Date	R	Opp.
BOS	Jun 8, 1950	29	STL
CHI	Apr 23, 1955	29	KC
CLE	Jul 7, 1923	27	BOS
CLE	Aug 12, 1948	26	STL
CLE	May 30, 1950	26	STL
CLE	May 11, 1930	25	PHI
NY	May 24, 1936	25	PHI
PHI	May 18, 1912	24	DET
NY	Sep 28, 1923	24	BOS
CLE	Jul 29, 1928	24	NY
PHI	May 1, 1929	24	BOS
PHI	May 6, 1929	24	BOS
BOS	Sep 27, 1940	24	WAS
BOS	Sep 27, 1944	24	PHI
TOR	Jun 26, 1978	24	BAL
CAL	Aug 25, 1979	24	TOR
BOS	May 2, 1901	23	PHI
CLE	Sep 2, 1902	23	BAL
BOS	Aug 26, 1937	23	CHI
NY	Jun 28, 1939	23	PHI
BOS	Jun 18, 1953	23	DET
KC	Apr 6, 1974	23	MIN
PHI	Jul 8, 1902	22	BOS
CLE	Aug 7, 1923	22	WAS
NY	Jul 26, 1931	22	CHI
NY	May 2, 1939	22	DET
BOS	Jun 29, 1950	22	PHI
NY	Aug 12, 1953	22	WAS
CHI	May 31, 1970	22	BOS

The Wrigley Field scoreboard on May 17, 1979—a scoreboard operator's nightmare.

Most Runs, Game, NL since 1900

Team	Date	R	Opp.
STL	Jul 6, 1929	28	PHI
BKN	Sep 24, 1901	26	CIN
CIN	Jun 4, 1911	26	BOS
CHI	Aug 25, 1922	26	PHI
NY	Apr 30, 1944	26	BKN
BKN	Sep 23, 1900	25	CIN
NY	Jun 9, 1901	25	CIN
BKN	Sep 23, 1901	25	CIN
CIN	May 13, 1902	24	PHI
PIT	Jun 22, 1925	24	STL
NY	Sep 2, 1925	24	PHI
CHI	Jul 3, 1945	24	BOS
PHI	Jul 13, 1900	23	PIT
PIT	Apr 27, 1912	23	CIN
PHI	Aug 25, 1922	23	CHI
STL	Sep 16, 1926	23	PHI
NY	Jul 11, 1931	23	PHI
CIN	Jun 8, 1940	23	BKN
BKN	Jul 10, 1943	23	PIT
CIN	Jul 6, 1949	23	CHI
CHI	Apr 17, 1954	23	STL
MIL	Sep 2, 1957	23	CHI
CIN	Apr 25, 1977	23	ATL
CHI	May 17, 1977	23	SD
PHI	May 17, 1979	23	CHI
NY	Jun 5, 1912	22	CIN
STL	Jul 27, 1918	22	BKN
NY	Jun 1, 1923	22	PHI
NY	Sep 10, 1924	22	BOS
BKN	Sep 6, 1930	22	PHI
BKN	Jul 29, 1936	22	STL
CHI	Aug 13, 1937	22	CIN
BKN	Sep 23, 1939	22	PHI
CIN	Jun 1, 1957	22	CHI
PIT	Sep 16, 1975	22	CHI
CHI	May 17, 1979	22	PHI

The greatest display of slugging power by any one team since 1900 was put on by the Boston Red Sox on June 8, 1950. The Red Sox battered the hapless St. Louis Browns 29–4, on 28 hits, including nine doubles, a triple, and seven home runs. They broke the post-1900 records for most runs (29), most total bases (60), and most extra-base hits (17). Including the previous day's 20–4 rout, also against the Browns, the Red Sox also established two-game marks for most runs (49) and most hits (51).

Most Hits, Game, AL

Team	Date	H	Opp.	Team	Date	H	Opp.
CLE	Jul 10, 1932	33	PHI	NY	Jun 20, 1932	26	PHI
NY	Aug 31, 1974	31	CHI	PHI	Jun 21, 1932	26	CHI
NY	Sep 28, 1923	30	BOS	CHI	Sep 11, 1936	26	PHI
PHI	May 3, 1929	29	BOS	KC	Jul 27, 1956	26	NY
CLE	Aug 12, 1948	29	STL	CAL	Aug 25, 1979	26	TOR
BOS	May 9, 1949	29	PHI	MIL	May 5, 1901	25	CHI
CHI	Apr 23, 1955	29	KC	DET	Jul 27, 1908	25	PHI
PHI	Aug 10, 1901	28	WAS	STL	Sep 12, 1909	25	DET
DET	Sep 29, 1928	28	NY	PHI	Sep 23, 1914	25	DET
BOS	Jun 8, 1950	28	STL	CHI	May 3, 1918	25	DET
NY	Aug 12, 1953	28	WAS	BOS	Sep 5, 1919	25	PHI
PHI	Aug 11, 1902	27	BOS	CHI	Aug 15, 1922	25	BOS
NY	Aug 31, 1921	27	WAS	PHI	Jul 25, 1929	25	CLE
CLE	Jul 29, 1928	27	NY	CLE	Jun 5, 1930	25	BOS
CLE	May 11, 1930	27	NY	CHI	Jul 10, 1932	25	CLE
WAS	May 16, 1933	27	CHI	NY	Jun 6, 1934	25	BOS
CLE	Apr 29, 1950	27	PHI	DET	Jul 1, 1936	25	CHI
BOS	Jun 18, 1953	27	DET	PHI	Jul 26, 1936	25	CLE
BOS	Apr 24, 1960	27	WAS	PHI	Jul 27, 1936	25	CHI
BOS	Aug 5, 1979	27	MIL	BOS	Jun 24, 1949	25	STL
PHI	May 18, 1912	26	DET	CLE	Apr 29, 1952	25	PHI
CLE	Aug 7, 1923	26	WAS	OAK	Jun 14, 1969	25	BOS

Most Hits, Game, NL since 1900

Team	Date	H	Opp.	Team	Date	H	Opp.
NY	Jun 9, 1901	31	CIN	NY	Aug 10, 1930	26	PHI
BKN	Jul 31, 1931	31	PHI	NY	May 13, 1957	26	BKN
NY	Sep 2, 1925	30	PHI	MIL	Sep 2, 1957	26	CHI
BKN	Sep 3, 1936	30	STL	SF	May 13, 1958	26	LA
BKN	Jun 25, 1900	28	NY	CHI	May 17, 1979	26	PHI
CIN	May 13, 1901	28	PHI	BOS	Apr 10, 1900	25	PHI
BKN	Aug 22, 1917	28	PIT	BKN	Jun 10, 1900	25	PHI
NY	Jul 10, 1922	28	PIT	BOS	Jun 25, 1900	25	PHI
NY	Jul 10, 1923	28	PIT	PHI	Jul 13, 1900	25	PIT
NY	Jun 15, 1929	28	PIT	PHI	Jun 4, 1901	25	CIN
STL	Jul 6, 1929	28	PHI	PHI	Jun 24, 1901	25	CIN
BKN	Jun 23, 1930	28	PIT	CIN	Jun 24, 1917	25	STL
NY	Jul 11, 1931	28	PHI	PIT	Jun 9, 1921	25	BOS
CHI	Jul 3, 1945	28	BOS	NY	May 30, 1922	25	BOS
MON	Jun 30, 1978	28	ATL	BKN	Jun 21, 1922	25	PIT
PIT	Apr 27, 1912	27	CIN	CHI	Aug 25, 1922	25	PHI
NY	Aug 5, 1922	27	CHI	PHI	Aug 25, 1922	25	CHI
PIT	Aug 8, 1922	27	PHI	BKN	Jun 29, 1923	25	PHI
NY	Sep 10, 1924	27	BOS	STL	Aug 24, 1924	25	BKN
PHI	Jul 23, 1930	27	PIT	PIT	Jun 20, 1925	25	BKN
NY	Sep 21, 1931	27	CHI	PIT	Jun 12, 1927	25	PHI
BKN	Sep 23, 1939	27	PHI	PIT	Jun 12, 1928	25	PHI
CIN	Jun 8, 1940	27	BKN	NY	Sep 2, 1930	25	PHI
STL	Aug 5, 1957	27	BKN	STL	Aug 9, 1932	25	PHI
PIT	Jul 31, 1900	26	BKN	PIT	Aug 25, 1936	25	STL
BKN	Jun 21, 1901	26	CIN	BKN	Jun 24, 1950	25	PIT
BKN	Sep 23, 1901	26	CIN	CIN	Aug 3, 1969	25	PHI
STL	Jul 27, 1918	26	BKN	STL	Jun 27, 1973	25	PIT
CIN	Jul 13, 1923	26	PHI	HOU	May 30, 1976	25	ATL
CHI	Sep 12, 1923	26	CIN	HOU	Jul 2, 1976	25	CIN
NY	Jul 10, 1930	26	PHI	MON	May 21, 1977	25	SD

Over 60 years ago, the Boston Braves and Brooklyn Dodgers engaged in the longest game in major league history, battling through 26 innings to a 1–1 tie. Umpire Barry McCormick finally had to call the game because of darkness. Today's excellent lighting would have allowed the game to continue, but Braves Field had no lights in those days. It was probably just as well for the pitchers, Joe Oeschger of the Braves and Leon Cadore of the Dodgers, that the game ended when it did. They both pitched all 26 innings and would no doubt have been expected to add to their already incredible marathon performances.

The following afternoon, the Dodgers dropped a 13-inning game to Philadelphia, then returned to Boston the next day for yet another extra-inning contest, this one won by the Braves in 19 innings. That made for an astounding total of 58 innings in three days without a victory. The Dodgers survived to win the pennant that year.

The Dodgers and Braves each used just 11 players in their 26-inning game. Forty-eight years later, the Mets and Cardinals played a 25-inning game, won by the Cardinals 4–3. The teams used a combined total of 50 players in that game, including 11 pitchers.

The Mets have played in two other marathon contests in their short history and lost them, too. They lost 8–6 to the Giants in 23 innings in the second game of a doubleheader in 1964, and they lost the longest 1–0 game in history, 24 innings, to the Astros in 1968. While these long games are hard on the players, they're even tougher for the umpires. The players get to sit down every half-inning, but the umpires are on their feet for every single pitch. Incredibly, the home-plate umpire in all three of the Mets' long games was Ed Sudol, who probably got very tired of the sight of the Mets' uniforms.

Longest Games, AL

Team	Date	Opp.	Inns.	Score
PHI	Sep 1, 1906	BOS	24	4-1
DET	Jul 21, 1945	PHI	24	1-1
NY	Jun 24, 1962	DET	22	9-7
WAS	Jun 12, 1967	CHI	22	6-5
MIL	May 12, 1972	MIN	22	4-3
DET	May 24, 1929	CHI	21	6-5
OAK	Jun 4, 1971	WAS	21	5-3
CHI	May 26, 1973	CLE	21	6-3
PHI	Jul 4, 1905	BOS	20	4-2
WAS	Aug 9, 1967	MIN	20	9-7
NY	Aug 29, 1967	BOS	20	4-3
BOS	Jul 27, 1969	SEA	20	5-3
OAK	Jul 9, 1971	CAL	20	1-0
WAS	Sep 14, 1971	CLE	20	8-6

Longest Games, NL

Team	Date	Opp.	Inns.	Score
BKN	May 1, 1920	BOS	26	1-1
STL	Sep 11, 1974	NY	25	4-3
HOU	Apr 15, 1968	NY	24	1-0
BKN	Jun 27, 1939	BOS	23	2-2
SF	May 31, 1964	NY	23	8-6
BKN	Aug 22, 1917	PIT	22	6-5
CHI	May 17, 1927	BOS	22	4-3
NY	Jul 17, 1914	PIT	21	3-1
CHI	Jul 17, 1918	PHI	21	2-1
PIT	Aug 1, 1918	BOS	21	2-0
SF	Sep 1, 1967	CIN	21	1-0
HOU	Sep 24, 1971	SD	21	2-1
SD	May 21, 1977	MON	21	11-8
CHI	Jun 30, 1892	CIN	20	7-7
CHI	Aug 24, 1905	PHI	20	2-1
BKN	Apr 30, 1919	PHI	20	9-9
STL	Aug 28, 1930	CHI	20	8-7
BKN	Jul 5, 1940	BOS	20	6-2
PHI	May 4, 1973	ATL	20	5-4
PIT	Jul 6, 1980	CHI	20	5-4
HOU	Aug 15, 1980	SD	20	3-1

Umpire **Ed Sudol,** the man who presided over the three longest games in New York Mets history: a 23-inning loss in 1964, a 24-inning loss in 1968, and a 25-inning loss in 1974.

Retired Numbers, AL

Player	Team	No.
Frank Robinson	BAL	20
Brooks Robinson	BAL	5
Ted Williams	BOS	9
Luke Appling	CHI	4
Nellie Fox	CHI	2
Lou Boudreau	CLE	5
Bob Feller	CLE	19
Earl Averill	CLE	3
Hank Aaron	MIL	44
Al Kaline	DET	6
Harmon Killebrew	MIN	3
Babe Ruth	NY	3
Lou Gehrig	NY	4
Joe DiMaggio	NY	5
Mickey Mantle	NY	7
Casey Stengel	NY	37
Bill Dickey	NY	8
Yogi Berra	NY	8
Whitey Ford	NY	16
Thurman Munson	NY	15

Roberto Clemente, the Pirate right-fielder for 18 seasons *(top left)*. Baltimore third baseman **Brooks Robinson** *(left)*. **Willie Mays** with the San Francisco Giants *(above)*.

Forty-seven players, coaches, and managers have had their uniform numbers permanently retired by their teams. Since numbers didn't appear on uniforms until 1929, such early greats as Ty Cobb, Tris Speaker, George Sisler, Walter Johnson, Cy Young, and Christy Mathewson had no numbers to retire. The numbers originally referred to a player's place in the batting order. Babe Ruth, who batted third for the Yankees, wore 3; Lou Gehrig, who followed him, wore 4.

Two men have had their numbers retired in both leagues. Casey Stengel's number 37 was retired by both the New York Yankees and the New York Mets. He had managed the Yankees when they were one of the best teams in baseball history, and he managed the Mets when they were one of the worst. Hank Aaron's number 44 was retired by the Braves and the Brewers. Aaron spent the last two years of his career with the Milwaukee Brewers, back in the city where he'd spent the bulk of his career.

Retired Numbers, NL

Player	Team	No.
Warren Spahn	ATL	21
Eddie Mathews	ATL	41
Hank Aaron	ATL	44
Fred Hutchinson	CIN	1
Jim Umbricht	HOU	32
Don Wilson	HOU	40
Jim Gilliam	LA	19
Walter Alston	LA	24
Sandy Koufax	LA	32
Roy Campanella	LA	39
Jackie Robinson	LA	42
Duke Snider	LA	4
Gil Hodges	NY	14
Casey Stengel	NY	37
Richie Ashburn	PHI	1
Robin Roberts	PHI	36
Billy Meyer	PIT	1
Pie Traynor	PIT	20
Roberto Clemente	PIT	21
Honus Wagner	PIT	33
Danny Murtaugh	PIT	40
Dizzy Dean	STL	17
Lou Brock	STL	20
Bob Gibson	STL	45
Stan Musial	STL	6
Carl Hubbell	SF	11
Mel Ott	SF	4
Willie Mays	SF	24
Juan Marichal	SF	27

Babe Ruth in his famed Yankee pin stripes.

Career Spent With One Team (18 or more years)

Player	Team	Yrs.	Pos.
Brooks Robinson	BAL A	23	3B
Cap Anson	CHI N	22	1B
Al Kaline	DET A	22	OF
Stan Musial	STL N	22	OF-1B
Mel Ott	NY N	22	OF
Fred Clarke	LOU N		
	PIT N	21	OF
Walter Johnson	WAS A	21	P
Ted Lyons	CHI A	21	P
Honus Wagner	LOU N		
	PIT N	21	SS
Luke Appling	CHI A	20	SS
Red Faber	CHI A	20	P
Mel Harder	CLE A	20	P
Carl Yastrzemski	BOS A	20	OF-1B
Ernie Banks	CHI N	19	SS-1B
Charlie Gehringer	DET A	19	2B
Willie Stargell	PIT N	19	OF-1B
Ted Williams	BOS A	19	OF
Ossie Bluege	WAS A	18	3B
Roberto Clemente	PIT N	18	OF
Bob Feller	CLE A	18	P
Ed Kranepool	NY N	18	1B-OF
Mickey Mantle	NY A	18	OF-1B

Stan "The Man" Musial spent 22 years with the St. Louis Cardinals. He hit .330 in 1962 to finish third in the National League—at the age of forty-one!

The Free Agent Explosion: 1970–Present

A fan who had fallen asleep in 1920 and awakened 60 years later would hardly recognize the game he once knew. Where there had been 16 teams, there were now 26. The game that had been played in sunlight on a grass field was now played mostly at night, often on a plastic surface known as "artificial turf." Starting pitchers no longer stayed in the game to the end; they were routinely replaced by a new breed of specialists: relief pitchers. In the American League, pitchers no longer even batted. They were replaced by a "designated hitter" who bats but does not play in the field. But the most startling change is the fact that ballplayers could again jump from one team to another in search of higher pay for the first time since the AL-NL peace treaty of 1903.

Since that treaty, a player's contract had bound him to one club for life. The club could sell or trade him, but he could not leave without retiring from the game. The new era came when an arbitrator ruled that when a player's contract expired, he was a free agent who could sign with any team he pleased. The new free-agent market led to ever higher salaries for baseball players. It also meant that a team owner could build a winning club by bidding for established stars instead of having to scout out and develop great players of his own.

While players moved to different teams, the teams themselves stayed pretty much where they were. The formerly new Washington Senators became the new Texas Rangers, and the American League expanded again to Toronto and Seattle (replacing the Pilots). The National League made no changes.

Many major records fell in the 1970s. Babe Ruth lost his other home-run record to Hank Aaron in 1974, as Aaron hit his 715th career home run. Never spectacular but always consistent, Aaron never hit more than 47 homers in a season. Lou Brock eclipsed Maury Wills's stolen-base record by stealing 118 bases in 1975 at the age of 35. Rod Carew and George Brett made runs at a .400 batting average; Carew finished at .388 in 1977, and Brett topped that with a .390 average in 1980. But the most dramatic blow was struck by Carlton Fisk of the Boston Red Sox against the Cincinnati Reds in the sixth game of the 1975 Series. Each team had fought back after trailing by three runs, and the score was tied in the twelfth inning. The clock had already struck midnight when Fisk lined a high drive down the left-field line. Millions of TV viewers saw Fisk wave his arms, urging the ball to stay fair. When it did, Fisk clapped his hands and ran joyously around the bases. The next night, a record *71 million* fans watched Cincinnati win the seventh game. That 1975 Series brought to a whole new audience the drama and beauty of the game of baseball and signaled its rebirth as America's #1 sport.

FREE AGENTS

When Oakland A's owner Charles O. Finley missed a payment on Catfish Hunter's contract, Hunter was declared a free agent. This set off a bidding war. Hunter signed with the Yankees *(top left),* who gave him baseball's first multimillion-dollar contract, ending forever the days when a $100,000-a-year salary was the mark of a truly great player. In 1980, Nolan Ryan *(bottom)* became the first $1,000,000-a-year pitcher when he signed with the Astros. A relative bargain, Steve Stone *(top right)* signed with the Orioles for a fraction of Ryan's salary and won the AL Cy Young Award in 1980.

THE MAN WITH THE MONEY

In the 1970s, baseball fans heard as much about big salaries as they did about batting averages. Dave Winfield's $25 million contract got far more attention than Mike Schmidt's 48 homers in 1980. The man who helped make the 1970s the money years was Yankee owner George Steinbrenner. Steinbrenner was willing to pay the highest salaries for the best players in an effort to make the Yankees a winning team. While many fans, sportswriters, and players don't like Steinbrenner's habit of complaining about the Yankees' playing and interfering with his managers, they have to admit that he made the Yankees the most talked-about team in the majors.

REGGIE JACKSON

Loud and outspoken, Reggie Jackson makes himself the center of attention wherever he goes. He was the top home-run hitter on the Oakland team that won the World Series in 1972, 1973, and 1974, but he didn't think he was getting enough recognition. "If I played in New York, they'd name a candy bar after me," he said. He became a free agent and signed with the Yankees. Despite the pressures he put on himself, Jackson showed that he was one of the best clutch hitters in baseball. His three home runs on three straight pitches clinched the 1977 World Series for the Yankees *(below)*, earned him the nickname "Mr. October," and led to a new candy bar called Reggie.

PETE ROSE

Pete Rose is a throwback—the kind of hustling, driving, hardworking ballplayer that old-timers say doesn't exist any more. He plays each game with every bit of effort he has, and he has kept it up for 18 years so far. Rose has truly earned the nickname "Charlie Hustle" for his all-out approach to the game. A student of baseball statistics, Rose keeps close track of his many records. He has more seasons with 200 or more hits, 10, than anyone else. His 44-game hitting streak in 1978 tied Willie Keeler's NL mark. He entered the 1981 season 634 hits shy of Ty Cobb's record of 4,191, and he seems determined to keep playing until he breaks it. A real leader, Rose is the most important ballplayer of his era.

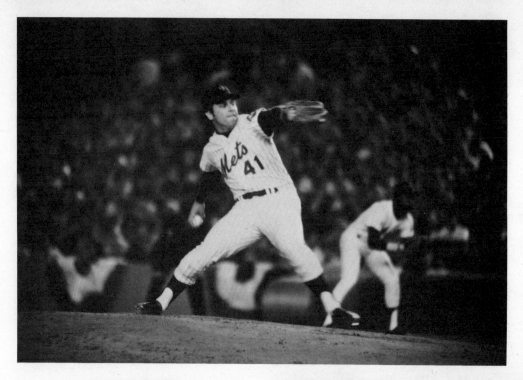

TOM SEAVER

When Tom Seaver joined the New York Mets in 1967, they had finished as high as ninth place just once. Two years later, he led them to a World Series victory over the Baltimore Orioles in one of the greatest upsets in baseball history. A power pitcher with a great fastball and good control, Seaver is the first pitcher to strike out 200 or more batters in nine straight seasons. He was traded by the Mets to the Cincinnati Reds in 1977. He returned to Shea Stadium for the first time that August, where he acknowledged the cheers of the crowd with a tip of his hat before pitching a six-hitter against his old club *(right)*.

Since 1876 there have been 275 brother combinations in baseball. The largest baseball family was the Delahantys. Five brothers—Ed, Jim, Joe, Tom, and Frank—made it to the majors.

Probably the best-known brother act was the DiMaggios—Joe, Dom, and Vince, all outfielders. But the only trio of brothers ever to appear together in one line-up was the Alou family. Felipe, Matty, and Jesus all played in the Giant outfield in a game on September 15, 1963.

The only brothers to win batting titles are Dixie and Harry Walker; Dixie hit .357 for the Dodgers in 1944, and Harry hit .373 for the Cardinals and Phillies in 1947. Other brotherly accomplishments: Bob and Ken Forsch are the only brothers to have pitched no-hitters; Gaylord and Jim Perry are the only brothers who have each won over 200 games; Bob and Irish Meusel are the only brothers to lead the league in RBIs; and Paul and Lloyd Waner are the only brothers in the Hall of Fame.

Perhaps the sweetest moment of brotherly revenge came on July 19, 1933. In the top of the fourth inning, Rick Ferrell hit a home run off brother Wes, who was pitching for the Indians. In the bottom of the fourth, Wes hit a home run on a pitch called by brother Rick, who was catching for the Red Sox.

Home Runs by Brothers in One Game

Player	Team	Date	Inn.	Opp.	Opp. Pitcher
Lloyd Waner	PIT N	Sep 4, 1927	5	CIN	Dolf Luque
Paul Waner	PIT N	Sep 4, 1927	5	CIN	
Paul Waner	PIT N	Jun 9, 1929	5	BKN	Doug McWeeny
Lloyd Waner	PIT N	Jun 9, 1929	7	BKN	
Rick Ferrell	BOS A	Jul 19, 1933	4	CLE	Wes Ferrell
Wes Ferrell	CLE A	Jul 19, 1933	4	BOS	Hank Johnson
Tony Cuccinello	BKN N	Jul 5, 1935	8	NY	Leon Chagnon
Al Cuccinello	NY N	Jul 5, 1935	9	BKN	Johnny Babich
Lloyd Waner	PIT N	Sep 15, 1938	5	NY	Cliff Melton
Paul Waner	PIT N	Sep 15, 1938	5	NY	Cliff Melton
Dom DiMaggio	BOS A	Jun 30, 1950	6	NY	Joe Ostrowski
Joe DiMaggio	NY A	Jun 30, 1950	8	BOS	Walt Masterson
Felipe Alou	SF N	May 15, 1961	1	CHI	Dick Ellsworth
Matty Alou	SF N	May 15, 1961	8	CHI	Joe Schaffernoth
Hank Aaron	MIL N	Jun 12, 1962	2	LA	Phil Ortega
Tommie Aaron	MIL N	Jun 12, 1962	8	LA	Ed Roebuck
Tommie Aaron	MIL N	Jul 12, 1962	9	STL	Larry Jackson
Hank Aaron	MIL N	Jul 12, 1962	9	STL	Lindy McDaniel
Tommie Aaron	MIL N	Aug 14, 1962	6	CIN	Johnny Klippstein
Hank Aaron	MIL N	Aug 14, 1962	7	CIN	Ted Wills
Jesus Alou	SF N	Aug 12, 1965	6	PIT	Bob Friend
Matty Alou	SF N	Aug 12, 1965	8	PIT	Don Schwall
Billy Conigliaro	BOS A	Jul 4, 1970	4	CLE	Steve Dunning
Tony Conigliaro	BOS A	Jul 4, 1970	7	CLE	Fred Lasher
Billy Conigliaro	BOS A	Sep 19, 1970	4	WAS	Jim Hannan
Tony Conigliaro	BOS A	Sep 19, 1970	7	WAS	Joe Grzenda
Graig Nettles	NY A	Sep 14, 1974	1	DET	Mickey Lolich
Jim Nettles	DET A	Sep 14, 1974	2	NY	Pat Dobson

Jesus, Matty, and **Felipe Alou** *(left to right)* played together for just one year with the Giants, but that was long enough for them to make up baseball's first all-brother outfield.

Three or More Brothers in Baseball

Player	First	Last	Player	First	Last
Richie Allen	1963	1977	Hugh High	1913	1918
Hank Allen	1965	1973	Charlie High	1919	1920
Ron Allen	1972	1972	Andy High	1922	1934
Felipe Alou	1958	1974	Mike Mansell	1879	1884
Matty Alou	1960	1974	Tom Mansell	1879	1884
Jesus Alou	1963	1979	John Mansell	1882	1882
Cloyd Boyer	1949	1955	Mike O'Neill	1901	1907
Ken Boyer	1955	1969	Jack O'Neill	1902	1906
Clete Boyer	1955	1971	Steve O'Neill	1911	1928
John Clarkson	1882	1894	Jim O'Neill	1920	1923
Dad Clarkson	1891	1896	Eddie Sadowski	1960	1966
Walter Clarkson	1904	1908	Ted Sadowski	1960	1962
Jose Cruz	1970		Bob Sadowski	1963	1966
Hector Cruz	1973		Joe Sewell	1920	1933
Cirilio Cruz	1973	1977	Luke Sewell	1921	1942
Ed Delahanty	1888	1903	Tommy Sewell	1927	1927
Tom Delahanty	1894	1897	Len Sowders	1886	1886
Jim Delahanty	1901	1915	John Sowders	1887	1890
Frank Delahanty	1905	1915	Bill Sowders	1888	1890
Joe Delahanty	1907	1909	George Wright	1876	1882
Joe DiMaggio	1936	1951	Sam Wright	1876	1881
Vince DiMaggio	1937	1946	Harry Wright	1876	1877
Dom DiMaggio	1940	1953			

Brothers with Most Home Runs, Career

Player	HR	Player	HR
Hank Aaron	755	Bill Dickey	202
Tommie Aaron	13	George Dickey	4
Total	768	Total	206
Joe DiMaggio	361	Charlie Keller	189
Vince DiMaggio	125	Hal Keller	1
Dom DiMaggio	87	Total	190
Total	573	Walker Cooper	173
Ken Boyer	282	Mort Cooper	6
Clete Boyer	162	Total	179
Total	444	Paul Waner	112
Lee May	351	Lloyd Waner	28
Carlos May	90	Total	140
Total	441	Roger Connor	136
Richie Allen	351	Joe Connor	1
Hank Allen	6	Total	137
Ron Allen	1	Zack Wheat	132
Total	358	Mack Wheat	4
Bob Johnson	288	Total	136
Roy Johnson	58	Gee Walker	124
Total	346	Hub Walker	5
Graig Nettles	280	Total	129
Jim Nettles	16	Ed Delahanty	100
Total	296	Jim Delahanty	18
Hank Sauer	288	Frank Delahanty	5
Ed Sauer	5	Joe Delahanty	4
Total	293	Total	127
Felipe Alou	206	Frank Bolling	106
Jesus Alou	32	Milt Bolling	19
Matty Alou	31	Total	125
Total	269	Gene Freese	115
Joe Torre	252	George Freese	3
Frank Torre	13	Total	118
Total	265	Dixie Walker	105
Bob Meusel	156	Harry Walker	10
Irish Meusel	106	Total	115
Total	262		
Tony Conigliaro	166		
Billy Conigliaro	40		
Total	206		

Best-Hitting Brothers

Player	Yrs.	G	H	2B	3B	HR	RBI	BA
Paul Waner	20	2549	3152	603	190	112	1309	.333
Lloyd Waner	18	1992	2459	281	118	28	598	.316
Total	38	4541	5611	884	308	140	1907	.325
Ed Delahanty	16	1835	2597	522	185	100	1464	.346
Jim Delahanty	13	1186	1159	191	60	18	489	.283
Frank Delahanty	6	287	223	22	82	5	94	.222
Joe Delahanty	3	269	222	30	15	4	100	.238
Tom Delahanty	3	19	16	5	0	0	6	.239
Total	41	3596	4217	770	282	127	2153	.311
Bob Meusel	11	1407	1693	368	95	156	1067	.309
Irish Meusel	11	1294	1521	250	92	107	820	.310
Total	22	2701	3214	618	187	263	1887	.309
Jim O'Rourke	19	1774	2304	414	132	51	830	.310
John O'Rourke	3	230	279	58	24	11	98	.285
Total	22	2004	2583	472	156	62	928	.309
Dixie Walker	18	1905	2064	376	96	105	1023	.306
Harry Walker	11	807	786	126	37	10	214	.296
Total	19	2712	2850	502	133	115	1237	.303
Hank Aaron	23	3298	3771	624	98	755	2297	.305
Tommie Aaron	7	437	216	42	6	13	94	.229
Total	30	3735	3987	666	104	768	2391	.300
Joe DiMaggio	13	1737	2219	389	131	361	1507	.325
Dom DiMaggio	11	1399	1680	308	57	87	618	.298
Vince DiMaggio	10	1110	959	209	24	125	584	.249
Total	34	4245	4853	906	212	573	2739	.297
Bob Johnson	13	1863	2051	396	95	288	1283	.296
Roy Johnson	10	1153	1292	275	83	58	556	.296
Total	23	3016	3343	671	178	346	1839	.296
Joe Sewell	14	1902	2226	436	68	49	1051	.312
Luke Sewell	20	1630	1393	273	56	20	696	.259
Tommy Sewell	1	1	0	0	0	0	0	.000
Total	35	3533	3619	709	124	69	1747	.292
Gee Walker	15	1783	1991	399	76	124	997	.294
Hub Walker	5	297	205	43	6	5	60	.263
Total	20	2080	2196	442	82	129	1057	.291
Richie Allen	15	1749	1848	320	79	351	1119	.292
Hank Allen	7	389	212	27	9	6	128	.241
Ron Allen	1	7	1	0	0	1	1	.091
Total	23	2145	2061	347	88	358	1248	.285
Felipe Alou	17	2082	2101	359	49	206	852	.286
Matty Alou	15	1667	1777	236	50	31	427	.307
Jesus Alou	15	1380	1216	170	27	32	377	.280
Total	47	5129	5094	765	126	269	1656	.280
Lee May	16	2003	1987	331	29	351	1224	.266
Carlos May	10	1165	1127	172	23	90	536	.274
Total	26	3168	3114	503	52	441	1260	.268

The Waner brothers were teammates in Pittsburgh for 14 years. **Lloyd "Little Poison" Waner** played center field; **Paul "Big Poison" Waner** played right. Paul's career batting average was .333; Lloyd hit .316. Paul *(right)* entered the Hall of Fame in 1952; Lloyd *(left)* joined him in 1967.

Eleven brother combinations have totaled 200 or more wins. One is currently active—Phil and Joe Niekro—but it's unlikely they'll break the record held by the Perrys, Jim and Gaylord. The Perrys have combined for 504 wins going into the 1981 season.

The single-season record is held by the Deans, Dizzy and Paul, who won 49 games for the 1934 Cardinals' "Gas House Gang."

There are 26 brother combinations with 100 or more big league wins. Most of them have the kind of imbalance shown by the Mathewson brothers. Christy won 373 games; brother Henry had a lifetime won-lost record of 0-1.

Most Wins by Brothers

Player	Yrs.	W	L
Gaylord Perry	19	289	230
Jim Perry	17	215	174
Total	36	504	404
John Clarkson	12	327	177
Dad Clarkson	6	39	39
Walter Clarkson	5	20	18
Total	23	386	234
Christy Mathewson	17	373	188
Henry Mathewson	2	0	1
Total	19	373	189
Phil Niekro	17	233	208
Joe Niekro	14	136	120
Total	31	369	328
Pud Galvin	14	361	309
Lou Galvin	1	0	2
Total	15	361	311
Old Hoss Radbourn	12	308	191
George Radbourn	1	1	2
Total	13	309	193
Stan Coveleski	14	217	141
Harry Coveleski	9	81	57
Total	23	298	198
Gus Weyhing	14	264	234
John Weyhing	2	3	4
Total	16	267	238
Will White	10	229	166
Deacon White	2	0	0
Total	12	229	166
Jesse Barnes	13	153	149
Virgil Barnes	9	61	59
Total	22	214	208
Dizzy Dean	12	150	83
Paul Dean	9	50	34
Total	21	200	117
Jeff Pfeffer	13	158	112
Big Jeff Pfeffer	6	31	40
Total	19	189	152

Most Wins by Brothers (continued)

Player	Yrs.	W	L
Larry Corcoran	8	177	90
Mike Corcoran	1	0	1
Total	9	177	91
Hooks Wiltse	12	141	90
Snake Wiltse	3	30	31
Total	15	171	121
Ken Forsch	11	78	81
Bob Forsch	7	82	68
Total	18	160	149
Lindy McDaniel	21	141	119
Von McDaniel	2	7	5
Total	23	148	124
Matt Kilroy	10	143	134
Mike Kilroy	2	0	3
Total	12	143	137
Rick Reuschel	9	125	114
Paul Reuschel	5	16	16
Total	14	141	130
Howie Camnitz	11	133	106
Harry Camnitz	2	1	0
Total	13	134	106
Long Tom Hughes	13	129	173
Ed Hughes	2	3	2
Total	15	132	175
Ad Gumbert	9	122	101
Billy Gumbert	3	7	8
Total	12	129	109
Frank Lary	12	128	116
Al Lary	3	0	1
Total	15	128	117
Frank Foreman	11	98	94
Brownie Foreman	2	11	13
Total	13	109	107
Johnny Morrison	10	103	80
Phil Morrison	1	0	0
Total	11	103	80
George Pipgras	11	102	73
Ed Pipgras	1	0	1
Total	12	102	74
Alex Kellner	12	101	112
Walt Kellner	2	0	0
Total	14	101	112

TEAM RECORDS

Brother Batteries, AL

Player	Team	Pos.	First	Last
Tommy Thompson	NY	P	1912	1912
Homer Thompson	NY	C		
Milt Gaston	BOS	P	1929	1929
Alex Gaston	BOS	C		
Wes Ferrell	BOS	P	1934	1937
Rick Ferrell	BOS	C		
Wes Ferrell	WAS	P	1937	1937
Rick Ferrell	WAS	C		
Bobby Shantz	PHI	P	1954	1954
Billy Shantz	PHI	C		
Bobby Shantz	KC	P	1955	1955
Billy Shantz	KC	C		
Bobby Shantz	NY	P	1960	1960
Billy Shantz	NY	C		

Brother Batteries, NL

Player	Team	Pos.	First	Last
Will White	BOS	P	1877	1877
Deacon White	BOS	C		
Will White	CIN	P	1878	1879
Deacon White	CIN	C		
Pete Wood	BUF	P	1885	1885
Fred Wood	BUF	C		
John Ewing	NY	P	1891	1891
Buck Ewing	NY	C		
Mike O'Neill	STL	P	1902	1903
Jack O'Neill	STL	C		
Lefty Tyler	BOS	P	1914	1914
Fred Tyler	BOS	C		
Mort Cooper	STL	P	1940	1945
Walker Cooper	STL	C		
Mort Cooper	NY	P	1947	1947
Walker Cooper	NY	C		
Elmer Riddle	CIN	P	1941	1941
Johnny Riddle	CIN	C		
Jim Bailey	CIN	P	1959	1959
Ed Bailey	CIN	C		
Larry Sherry	LA	P	1959	1962
Norm Sherry	LA	C		

Lou Gehrig and **Babe Ruth** *(opposite page, left to right)*. These two fearsome sluggers combined for 783 home runs in their ten seasons together. Their best year was 1927, when they hit 107 homers, drove in 339 runs, batted .365, and had a slugging percentage of .769.

The most famous one-two punch in baseball history is Babe Ruth and Lou Gehrig. They formed the heart of the fearsome Yankee batting order for ten years, but they no longer hold either the single-season or career record for home runs by two teammates. The single-season mark fell in 1961, the year Roger Maris broke Ruth's mark of 60. That year Maris and Yankee teammate Mickey Mantle combined for 114 homers. Their career mark has been passed twice, by Hank Aaron and Eddie Mathews of the Braves and by Willie Mays and Willie McCovey of the Giants.

Best Home Run Duos, Career, AL

Player	Team	First	Last	HR
Babe Ruth	NY	1925	1934	434
Lou Gehrig	NY	1925	1934	349
Total				783
Mickey Mantle	NY	1951	1963	419
Yogi Berra	NY	1951	1963	283
Total				702
Norm Cash	DET	1960	1974	373
Al Kaline	DET	1960	1974	274
Total				647
Harmon Killebrew	MIN	1962	1974	429
Tony Oliva	MIN	1962	1974	206
Total				635
Ted Williams	BOS	1939	1951	333
Bobby Doerr	BOS	1939	1951	216
Total				549
Norm Cash	DET	1963	1974	275
Willie Horton	DET	1963	1974	223
Total				498
Hank Greenberg	DET	1934	1945	250
Rudy York	DET	1934	1945	239
Total				489
Mickey Mantle	NY	1960	1966	216
Roger Maris	NY	1960	1966	203
Total				419
Joe DiMaggio	NY	1939	1949	210
Charlie Keller	NY	1939	1949	184
Total				394
Al Simmons	PHI	1925	1932	208
Jimmie Foxx	PHI	1925	1932	174
Total				382
Jim Rice	BOS	1974	1980	197
Fred Lynn	BOS	1974	1980	114
Total				311
Hal Trosky	CLE	1933	1939	180
Earl Averill	CLE	1933	1939	127
Total				307

Best Home Run Duos, Career, NL

Player	Team	First	Last	HR
Hank Aaron	MIL	1954	1966	442
Eddie Mathews	MIL	1954	1966	415
Total				857
Willie Mays	SF	1959	1971	430
Willie McCovey	SF	1959	1971	370
Total				800
Duke Snider	BKN	1947	1961	384
Gil Hodges	BKN	1947	1961	361
Total				745
Ernie Banks	CHI	1959	1971	329
Billy Williams	CHI	1959	1971	315
Total				644
Mike Schmidt	PHI	1972	1980	283
Greg Luzinski	PHI	1972	1980	220
Total				503
Johnny Bench	CIN	1971		275
George Foster	CIN	1971		222
Total				497
Willie Stargell	PIT	1962	1972	277
Roberto Clemente	PIT	1962	1972	185
Total				462
Ted Kluszewski	CIN	1949	1957	229
Wally Post	CIN	1949	1957	208
Total				437
Mel Ott	NY	1926	1936	265
Bill Terry	NY	1926	1936	138
Total				403
Ken Boyer	STL	1955	1963	218
Stan Musial	STL	1955	1963	183
Total				401

The ideal batting order would have to have a balance of left- and right-handed batters. The ideal pitching staff needs this kind of balance, too. It's rare to find a great pitching staff that doesn't have at least one strong pitcher from each side. While the career win totals below may not reflect this, the greatest of all lefty-righty combinations was probably Sandy Koufax and Don Drysdale.

Koufax and Drysdale were teammates from 1956 to 1966. For the first five years, though, Koufax struggled to control his blazing fastball. Once he did, he became one of the greatest pitchers the game has ever known. Drysdale was also a hard thrower, with a reputation for firing fastballs at the heads of batters who tried to stand too close to the plate. In the six seasons from 1961 to 1966, Koufax won 129 games, and Drysdale won 111, a combined average of 40 wins a year. Their best year together was 1965, when they combined for 49 wins, 15 shutouts, and 592 strikeouts. Koufax's record that year was 26–8; Drysdale's was 23–12.

Koufax's career was cut short by a painfully sore left elbow. He retired in 1966 at age 30, one of the greatest left-handed pitchers in the history of the game.

Sandy Koufax (left) and **Don Drysdale,** the Dodgers' deadly lefty-righty combination.

Best Lefty-Righty Duos

Player	Team	LH/RH	First	Last	W	L
Hooks Wiltse	NY N	LH	1904	1914	138	85
Christy Mathewson	NY N	RH	1904	1914	300	138
Total					438	223
Eddie Plank	PHI A	LH	1903	1914	228	124
Chief Bender	PHI A	RH	1903	1914	191	103
Total					419	227
Lefty Gomez	NY A	LH	1930	1942	189	101
Red Ruffing	NY A	RH	1930	1942	219	120
Total					408	221
Warren Spahn	MIL N	LH	1953	1963	228	125
Lew Burdette	MIL N	RH	1953	1963	178	109
Total					406	234
Carl Hubbell	NY N	LH	1931	1942	214	121
Hal Schumacher	NY N	RH	1931	1942	154	116
Total					368	237
Hal Newhouser	DET A	LH	1939	1952	202	147
Dizzy Trout	DET A	RH	1939	1952	161	153
Total					363	300
Curt Simmons	PHI N	LH	1948	1960	114	110
Robin Roberts	PHI N	RH	1948	1960	233	188
Total					347	298
Sandy Koufax	BKN N LA N	LH	1956	1966	163	85
Don Drysdale	BKN N LA N	RH	1956	1966	177	134
Total					340	219
Wilbur Cooper	PIT N	LH	1912	1924	202	159
Babe Adams	PIT N	RH	1912	1924	134	105
Total					336	264
Doc White	CHI A	LH	1904	1913	143	108
Ed Walsh	CHI A	RH	1904	1913	190	121
Total					333	229
Jerry Koosman	NY N	LH	1967	1977	137	122
Tom Seaver	NY N	RH	1967	1977	189	110
Total					326	232
Carl Hubbell	NY N	LH	1928	1937	192	102
Freddie Fitzsimmons	NY N	RH	1928	1937	133	91
Total					325	193
Bill Sherdel	STL N	LH	1920	1930	142	110
Jesse Haines	STL N	RH	1920	1930	166	127
Total					308	237
Rube Marquard	NY N	LH	1908	1915	195	89
Christy Mathewson	NY N	RH	1908	1915	103	80
Total					298	169
Hal Newhouser	DET A	LH	1941	1952	190	137
Virgil Trucks	DET A	RH	1941	1952	108	91
Total					298	228
Dave McNally	BAL A	LH	1965	1974	164	95
Jim Palmer	BAL A	RH	1965	1974	129	69
Total					293	164

Best Lefty-Righty Duos (continued)

Player	Team	LH/RH	First	Last	W	L
Eppa Rixey	CIN N	LH	1921	1929	155	110
Dolf Luque	CIN N	RH	1921	1929	125	137
Total					280	247
Johnny Vander Meer	CIN N	LH	1938	1948	108	101
Bucky Walters	CIN N	RH	1938	1948	160	107
Total					268	208
Herb Pennock	NY A	LH	1923	1930	145	75
Waite Hoyt	NY A	RH	1923	1930	119	73
Total					264	148
Tommy Bridges	DET A	LH	1933	1942	154	100
Schoolboy Rowe	DET A	RH	1933	1942	105	62
Total					259	162
Lefty Grove	PHI A	LH	1928	1933	152	41
George Earnshaw	PHI A	RH	1928	1933	98	58
Total					250	99
Ed Killian	DET A	LH	1904	1910	98	74
George Mullin	DET A	RH	1904	1910	136	114
Total					234	188
Mickey Lolich	DET A	LH	1963	1970	116	93
Denny McLain	DET A	RH	1963	1970	117	62
Total					233	155
Eppa Rixey	PHI N	LH	1912	1917	70	69
Grover Alexander	PHI N	RH	1912	1917	162	75
Total					232	144
Doc White	CHI A	LH	1904	1910	123	80
Frank Smith	CHI A	RH	1904	1910	108	81
Total					231	161
Ed Lopat	NY A	LH	1948	1954	109	51
Allie Reynolds	NY A	RH	1948	1954	112	57
Total					221	108

Awards
and
World
Series

World Series

Year	Winning Team	Score in Games	Losing Team	Year	Winning Team	Score in Games	Losing Team
1903	Boston (AL)	5-3	Pittsburgh (NL)	1942	St. Louis (NL)	4-1	New York (AL)
1904	No World Series			1943	New York (AL)	4-1	St. Louis (NL)
1905	New York (NL)	4-1	Philadelphia (AL)	1944	St. Louis (NL)	4-2	St. Louis (AL)
1906	Chicago (AL)	4-2	Chicago (NL)	1945	Detroit (AL)	4-3	Chicago (NL)
1907	Chicago (NL)	4-0	Detroit (AL)	1946	St. Louis (NL)	4-3	Boston (AL)
1908	Chicago (NL)	4-1	Detroit (AL)	1947	New York (AL)	4-3	Brooklyn (NL)
1909	Pittsburgh (NL)	4-3	Detroit (AL)	1948	Cleveland (AL)	4-2	Boston (NL)
1910	Philadelphia (AL)	4-1	Chicago (NL)	1949	New York (AL)	4-1	Brooklyn (NL)
1911	Philadelphia (AL)	4-2	New York (NL)	1950	New York (AL)	4-0	Philadelphia (NL)
1912	Boston (AL)	4-3	New York (NL)	1951	New York (AL)	4-2	New York (NL)
1913	Philadelphia (AL)	4-1	New York (NL)	1952	New York (AL)	4-3	Brooklyn (NL)
1914	Boston (NL)	4-0	Philadelphia (AL)	1953	New York (AL)	4-2	Brooklyn (NL)
1915	Boston (AL)	4-1	Philadelphia (NL)	1954	New York (NL)	4-0	Cleveland (AL)
1916	Boston (AL)	4-1	Brooklyn (NL)	1955	Brooklyn (NL)	4-3	New York (AL)
1917	Chicago (AL)	4-2	New York (NL)	1956	New York (AL)	4-3	Brooklyn (NL)
1918	Boston (AL)	4-2	Chicago (NL)	1957	Milwaukee (NL)	4-3	New York (AL)
1919	Cincinnati (NL)	5-3	Chicago (AL)	1958	New York (AL)	4-3	Milwaukee (NL)
1920	Cleveland (AL)	5-2	Brooklyn (NL)	1959	Los Angeles (NL)	4-3	Chicago (AL)
1921	New York (NL)	5-3	New York (AL)	1960	Pittsburgh (NL)	4-3	New York (AL)
1922	New York (NL)	4-0	New York (AL)	1961	New York (AL)	4-1	Cincinnati (NL)
1923	New York (AL)	4-2	New York (NL)	1962	New York (AL)	4-3	San Francisco (NL)
1924	Washington (AL)	4-3	New York (NL)	1963	Los Angeles (NL)	4-0	New York (AL)
1925	Pittsburgh (NL)	4-3	Washington (AL)	1964	St. Louis (NL)	4-3	New York (AL)
1926	St. Louis (NL)	4-3	New York (AL)	1965	Los Angeles (NL)	4-3	Minnesota (AL)
1927	New York (AL)	4-0	Pittsburgh (NL)	1966	Baltimore (AL)	4-0	Los Angeles (NL)
1928	New York (AL)	4-0	St. Louis (NL)	1967	St. Louis (NL)	4-3	Boston (AL)
1929	Philadelphia (AL)	4-1	Chicago (NL)	1968	Detroit (AL)	4-3	St. Louis (NL)
1930	Philadelphia (AL)	4-2	St. Louis (NL)	1969	New York (NL)	4-1	Baltimore (AL)
1931	St. Louis (NL)	4-3	Philadelphia (AL)	1970	Baltimore (AL)	4-1	Cincinnati (NL)
1932	New York (AL)	4-0	Chicago (NL)	1971	Pittsburgh (NL)	4-3	Baltimore (AL)
1933	New York (NL)	4-1	Washington (AL)	1972	Oakland (AL)	4-3	Cincinnati (NL)
1934	St. Louis (NL)	4-3	Detroit (AL)	1973	Oakland (AL)	4-3	New York (NL)
1935	Detroit (AL)	4-2	Chicago (NL)	1974	Oakland (AL)	4-1	Los Angeles (NL)
1936	New York (AL)	4-2	New York (NL)	1975	Cincinnati (NL)	4-3	Boston (AL)
1937	New York (AL)	4-1	New York (NL)	1976	Cincinnati (NL)	4-0	New York (AL)
1938	New York (AL)	4-0	Chicago (NL)	1977	New York (AL)	4-2	Los Angeles (NL)
1939	New York (AL)	4-0	Cincinnati (NL)	1978	New York (AL)	4-2	Los Angeles (NL)
1940	Cincinnati (NL)	4-3	Detroit (AL)	1979	Pittsburgh (NL)	4-3	Baltimore (AL)
1941	New York (AL)	4-1	Brooklyn (NL)	1980	Philadelphia (NL)	4-2	Kansas City (AL)

Most Valuable Players

The Most Valuable Player in each league is selected annually by the Baseball Writers Association. The award recognizes outstanding performance and the player's contribution to his team's success. The MVP was originally named by the Chalmers Automobile Company, which gave the winner a car, and then by the National and American Leagues.

NATIONAL LEAGUE			AMERICAN LEAGUE
		CHALMERS	
1911	Frank Schulte, Chicago (OF)	1911	Ty Cobb, Detroit (OF)
1912	Larry Doyle, New York (2B)	1912	Tris Speaker, Boston (OF)
1913	Jake Daubert, Brooklyn (1B)	1913	Walter Johnson, Washington (P)
1914	Johnny Evers, Boston (2B)	1914	Eddie Collins, Philadelphia (2B)
		LEAGUE	
1922	No Selection	1922	George Sisler, St. Louis (1B)
1923	No Selection	1923	Babe Ruth, New York (OF)
1924	Dazzy Vance, Brooklyn (P)	1924	Walter Johnson, Washington (P)
1925	Rogers Hornsby, St. Louis (2B)	1925	Roger Peckinpaugh, Washington (SS)
1926	Bob O'Farrell, St. Louis (C)	1926	George Burns, Cleveland (1B)
1927	Paul Waner, Pittsburgh (OF)	1927	Lou Gehrig, New York (1B)
1928	Jim Bottomley, St. Louis (1B)	1928	Mickey Cochrane, Philadelphia (C)
1929	Rogers Hornsby, Chicago (2B)	1929	No Selection

BASEBALL WRITERS ASSOCIATION OF AMERICA

1931	Frankie Frisch, St. Louis (2B)	1931	Lefty Grove, Philadelphia (P)
1932	Chuck Klein, Philadelphia (OF)	1932	Jimmie Foxx, Philadelphia (1B)
1933	Carl Hubbell, New York (P)	1933	Jimmie Foxx, Philadelphia (1B)
1934	Dizzy Dean, St. Louis (P)	1934	Mickey Cochrane, Detroit (C)
1935	Gabby Hartnett, Chicago (C)	1935	Hank Greenberg, Detroit (1B)
1936	Carl Hubbell, New York (P)	1936	Lou Gehrig, New York (1B)
1937	Joe Medwick, St. Louis (OF)	1937	Charlie Gehringer, Detroit (2B)
1938	Ernie Lombardi, Cincinnati (C)	1938	Jimmie Foxx, Boston (1B)
1939	Bucky Walters, Cincinnati (P)	1939	Joe DiMaggio, New York (OF)
1940	Frank McCormick, Cincinnati (1B)	1940	Hank Greenberg, Detroit (1B)
1941	Dolph Camilli, Brooklyn (1B)	1941	Joe DiMaggio, New York (OF)
1942	Mort Cooper, St. Louis (P)	1942	Joe Gordon, New York (2B)
1943	Stan Musial, St. Louis (OF)	1943	Spud Chandler, New York (P)

NATIONAL LEAGUE		AMERICAN LEAGUE	
1944	Marty Marion, St. Louis (SS)	1944	Hal Newhouser, Detroit (P)
1945	Phil Cavarretta, Chicago (1B)	1945	Hal Newhouser, Detroit (P)
1946	Stan Musial, St. Louis (1B)	1946	Ted Williams, Boston (OF)
1947	Bob Elliott, Boston (3B)	1947	Joe DiMaggio, New York (OF)
1948	Stan Musial, St. Louis (OF)	1948	Lou Boudreau, Cleveland (SS)
1949	Jackie Robinson, Brooklyn (2B)	1949	Ted Williams, Boston (OF)
1950	Jim Konstanty, Philadelphia (P)	1950	Phil Rizzuto, New York (SS)
1951	Roy Campanella, Brooklyn (C)	1951	Yogi Berra, New York (C)
1952	Hank Sauer, Chicago (OF)	1952	Bobby Shantz, Philadelphia (P)
1953	Roy Campanella, Brooklyn (C)	1953	Al Rosen, Cleveland (3B)
1954	Willie Mays, New York (OF)	1954	Yogi Berra, New York (C)
1955	Roy Campanella, Brooklyn (C)	1955	Yogi Berra, New York (C)
1956	Don Newcombe, Brooklyn (P)	1956	Mickey Mantle, New York (OF)
1957	Henry Aaron, Milwaukee (OF)	1957	Mickey Mantle, New York (OF)
1958	Ernie Banks, Chicago (SS)	1958	Jackie Jensen, Boston (OF)
1959	Ernie Banks, Chicago (SS)	1959	Nellie Fox, Chicago (2B)
1960	Dick Groat, Pittsburgh (SS)	1960	Roger Maris, New York (OF)
1961	Frank Robinson, Cincinnati (OF)	1961	Roger Maris, New York (OF)
1962	Maury Wills, Los Angeles (SS)	1962	Mickey Mantle, New York (OF)
1963	Sandy Koufax, Los Angeles (P)	1963	Elston Howard, New York (C)
1964	Ken Boyer, St. Louis (3B)	1964	Brooks Robinson, Baltimore (3B)
1965	Willie Mays, San Francisco (OF)	1965	Zoilo Versalles, Minnesota (SS)
1966	Roberto Clemente, Pittsburgh (OF)	1966	Frank Robinson, Baltimore (OF)
1967	Orlando Cepeda, St. Louis (1B)	1967	Carl Yastrzemski, Boston (OF)
1968	Bob Gibson, St. Louis (P)	1968	Denny McLain, Detroit (P)
1969	Willie McCovey, San Francisco (1B)	1969	Harmon Killebrew, Minnesota (3B)
1970	Johnny Bench, Cincinnati (C)	1970	Boog Powell, Baltimore (1B)
1971	Joe Torre, St. Louis (3B)	1971	Vida Blue, Oakland (P)
1972	Johnny Bench, Cincinnati (C)	1972	Richie Allen, Chicago (1B)
1973	Pete Rose, Cincinnati (OF)	1973	Reggie Jackson, Oakland (OF)
1974	Steve Garvey, Los Angeles (1B)	1974	Jeff Burroughs, Texas (OF)
1975	Joe Morgan, Cincinnati (2B)	1975	Fred Lynn, Boston (OF)
1976	Joe Morgan, Cincinnati (2B)	1976	Thurman Munson, New York (C)
1977	George Foster, Cincinnati (OF)	1977	Rod Carew, Minnesota (1B)
1978	Dave Parker, Pittsburgh (OF)	1978	Jim Rice, Boston (OF)
1979	Keith Hernandez, St. Louis (1B)	1979	Don Baylor, California (OF-DH)
	Willie Stargell, Pittsburgh (1B)	1980	George Brett, Kansas City (3B)
1980	Mike Schmidt, Philadelphia (3B)		

Cy Young Award Winners

(one selection 1956-66)

The Cy Young Award goes to the outstanding pitcher in each league. It is also voted by the Baseball Writers Association.

NATIONAL LEAGUE		AMERICAN LEAGUE	
1956	Don Newcombe, Brooklyn (RH)	1958	Bob Turley, New York (RH)
1957	Warren Spahn, Milwaukee (LH)	1959	Early Wynn, Chicago (RH)
1960	Vernon Law, Pittsburgh (RH)	1961	Whitey Ford, New York (LH)
1962	Don Drysdale, Los Angeles (RH)	1964	Dean Chance, Los Angeles (RH)
1963	Sandy Koufax, Los Angeles (LH)	1967	Jim Lonborg, Boston (RH)
1965	Sandy Koufax, Los Angeles (LH)	1968	Denny McLain, Detroit (RH)
1966	Sandy Koufax, Los Angeles (LH)	1969	Mike Cuellar, Baltimore (LH)
1967	Mike McCormick, San Francisco (LH)		Denny McLain, Detroit (RH)
1968	Bob Gibson, St. Louis (RH)	1970	Jim Perry, Minnesota (RH)
1969	Tom Seaver, New York (RH)	1971	Vida Blue, Oakland (LH)
1970	Bob Gibson, St. Louis (RH)	1972	Gaylord Perry, Cleveland (RH)
1971	Ferguson Jenkins, Chicago (RH)	1973	Jim Palmer, Baltimore (RH)
1972	Steve Carlton, Philadelphia (LH)	1974	Jim (Catfish) Hunter, Oakland (RH)
1973	Tom Seaver, New York (RH)	1975	Jim Palmer, Baltimore (RH)
1974	Mike Marshall, Los Angeles (RH)	1976	Jim Palmer, Baltimore (RH)
1975	Tom Seaver, New York (RH)	1977	Sparky Lyle, New York (LH)
1976	Randy Jones, San Diego (LH)	1978	Ron Guidry, New York (LH)
1977	Steve Carlton, Phidadelphia (LH)	1979	Mike Flanagan, Baltimore (LH)
1978	Gaylord Perry, San Diego (RH)	1980	Steve Stone, Baltimore (RH)
1979	Bruce Sutter, Chicago (RH)		
1980	Steve Carlton, Philadelphia (LH)		

Rookies of the Year
(one selection 1947-48)

The Rookie of the Year award is presented by the Baseball Writers Association.

NATIONAL LEAGUE

1947	Jackie Robinson, Brooklyn (1B)
1948	Alvin Dark, Boston (SS)
1949	Don Newcombe, Brooklyn (P)
1950	Sam Jethroe, Boston (OF)
1951	Willie Mays, New York (OF)
1952	Joe Black, Brooklyn (P)
1953	Junior Gilliam, Brooklyn (2B)
1954	Wally Moon, St. Louis (OF)
1955	Bill Virdon, St. Louis (OF)
1956	Frank Robinson, Cincinnati (OF)
1957	Jack Sanford, Philadelphia (P)
1958	Orlando Cepeda, San Francisco (1B)
1959	Willie McCovey, San Francisco (1B)
1960	Frank Howard, Los Angeles (OF)
1961	Billy Williams, Chicago (OF)
1962	Ken Hubbs, Chicago (2B)
1963	Pete Rose, Cincinnati (2B)
1964	Richie Allen, Philadelphia (3B)
1965	Jim Lefebvre, Los Angeles (2B)
1966	Tommy Helms, Cincinnati (2B)
1967	Tom Seaver, New York (P)
1968	Johnny Bench, Cincinnati (C)
1969	Ted Sizemore, Los Angeles (2B)
1970	Carl Morton, Montreal (P)
1971	Earl Williams, Atlanta (C)
1972	Jon Matlack, New York (P)
1973	Gary Matthews, San Francisco (OF)
1974	Bake McBride, St. Louis (OF)
1975	John Montefusco, San Francisco (P)
1976	Pat Zachry, Cincinnati (P)
	Butch Metzger, San Diego (P)
1977	Andre Dawson, Montreal (OF)
1978	Bob Horner, Atlanta (3B)
1979	Rick Sutcliffe, Los Angeles (P)
1980	Steve Howe, Los Angeles (P)

AMERICAN LEAGUE

1949	Roy Sievers, St. Louis (OF)
1950	Walt Dropo, Boston (1B)
1951	Gil McDougald, New York (3B)
1952	Harry Byrd, Philadelphia (P)
1953	Harvey Kuenn, Detroit (SS)
1954	Bob Grim, New York (P)
1955	Herb Score, Cleveland (P)
1956	Luis Aparicio, Chicago (SS)
1957	Tony Kubek, New York (SS)
1958	Albie Pearson, Washington (OF)
1959	Bob Allison, Washington (OF)
1960	Ron Hansen, Baltimore (SS)
1961	Don Schwall, Boston (P)
1962	Tom Tresh, New York (SS)
1963	Gary Peters, Chicago (P)
1964	Tony Oliva, Minnesota (OF)
1965	Curt Blefary, Baltimore (OF)
1966	Tommie Agee, Chicago (OF)
1967	Rod Carew, Minnesota (2B)
1968	Stan Bahnsen, New York (P)
1969	Lou Piniella, Kansas City (OF)
1970	Thurman Munson, New York (C)
1971	Chris Chambliss, Cleveland (1B)
1972	Carlton Fisk, Boston (C)
1973	Al Bumbry, Baltimore (OF)
1974	Mike Hargrove, Texas (1B)
1975	Fred Lynn, Boston (OF)
1976	Mark Fidrych, Detroit (P)
1977	Eddie Murray, Baltimore (DH)
1978	Lou Whitaker, Detroit (2B)
1979	Alfredo Griffin, Toronto (SS)
	John Castino, Minnesota (3B)
1980	Joe Charboneau, Cleveland (OF)

Baseball Hall of Fame

PLAYER	Career Dates	Year Selected	PLAYER	Career Dates	Year Selected
Grover Alexander	1911-1930	1938	Jesse Burkett	1890-1905	1946
Cap Anson	1876-1897	1939	Roy Campanella	1948-1957	1969
Luke Appling	1930-1950	1964	Max Carey	1910-1929	1961
Earl Averill	1929-1941	1975	Frank Chance	1898-1914	1946
J. Frank Baker	1908-1922	1955	Oscar Charleston*		1976
Dave Bancroft	1915-1930	1971	Jack Chesbro	1899-1909	1946
Ernie Banks	1953-1971	1977	Fred Clarke	1894-1915	1945
Jake Beckley	1888-1907	1971	John Clarkson	1882-1894	1963
James "Cool Papa" Bell*		1974	Roberto Clemente	1955-1972	1973
Chief Bender	1903-1925	1938	Ty Cobb	1905-1928	1936
Yogi Berra	1946-1965	1971	Mickey Cochrane	1925-1937	1947
Jim Bottomley	1922-1937	1974	Eddie Collins	1906-1930	1939
Lou Boudreau	1938-1952	1970	Jimmy Collins	1895-1908	1945
Roger Bresnahan	1897-1915	1945	Earle Combs	1924-1935	1970
Dan Brouthers	1879-1904	1945	Roger Connor	1880-1897	1976
Mordecai Brown	1903-1916	1949	Stan Coveleski	1912-1928	1969
			Sam Crawford	1899-1917	1957

Career Dates indicate first and last appearances in the majors.
*Elected on the basis of his career in the Negro Leagues.

PLAYER	Career Dates	Year Selected	PLAYER	Career Dates	Year Selected
Joe Cronin	1926-1945	1956	Tim Keefe	1880-1893	1964
Kiki Cuyler	1921-1938	1968	Willie Keeler	1892-1910	1939
Dizzy Dean	1930-1947	1953	Joe Kelley	1891-1908	1971
Ed Delahanty	1888-1903	1945	George Kelly	1915-1932	1973
Bill Dickey	1928-1946	1954	King Kelly	1878-1893	1945
Martin DiHigo*		1977	Ralph Kiner	1946-1955	1975
Joe DiMaggio	1936-1951	1955	Chuck Klein	1928-1944	1979
Hugh Duffy	1888-1906	1945	Sandy Koufax	1955-1966	1971
Johnny Evers	1902-1929	1946	Nap Lajoie	1896-1916	1937
Buck Ewing	1880-1897	1946	Bob Lemon	1941-1958	1976
Red Faber	1914-1933	1964	Buck Leonard*		1972
Bob Feller	1936-1956	1962	Fred Lindstrom	1924-1936	1976
Elmer Flick	1898-1910	1963	John Henry Lloyd*		1977
Whitey Ford	1950-1967	1974	Ted Lyons	1923-1946	1955
Jimmie Foxx	1925-1945	1951	Mickey Mantle	1951-1968	1974
Frank Frisch	1919-1937	1947	Heinie Manush	1923-1939	1964
Pud Galvin	1879-1892	1965	Rabbit Maranville	1912-1935	1954
Lou Gehrig	1923-1939	1939	Rube Marquard	1908-1925	1971
Charlie Gehringer	1924-1942	1949	Eddie Mathews	1952-1968	1978
Bob Gibson	1959-1975	1981	Christy Mathewson	1900-1916	1936
Josh Gibson*		1972	Willie Mays	1951-1973	1979
Lefty Gomez	1930-1943	1972	Tommy McCarthy	1884-1896	1946
Goose Goslin	1921-1938	1968	Joe McGinnity	1899-1908	1946
Hank Greenberg	1930-1947	1956	Joe Medwick	1932-1948	1968
Burleigh Grimes	1916-1934	1964	Johnny Mize	1936-1953	1981
Lefty Grove	1925-1941	1947	Stan Musial	1941-1963	1969
Chick Hafey	1924-1937	1971	Kid Nichols	1890-1906	1949
Jesse Haines	1918-1937	1970	Jim O'Rourke	1876-1904	1945
Billy Hamilton	1888-1901	1961	Mel Ott	1926-1947	1951
Gabby Hartnett	1922-1941	1955	Satchel Paige*	1948-1965	1971
Harry Heilmann	1914-1932	1952	Herb Pennock	1912-1934	1948
Billy Herman	1931-1947	1975	Eddie Plank	1901-1917	1946
Harry Hooper	1909-1925	1971	Hoss Radbourn	1880-1891	1939
Rogers Hornsby	1915-1937	1942	Sam Rice	1915-1934	1963
Waite Hoyt	1918-1938	1969	Eppa Rixey	1912-1933	1963
Carl Hubbell	1928-1943	1947	Robin Roberts	1948-1966	1976
Monte Irvin*	1949-1956	1973	Jackie Robinson	1947-1956	1962
Hugh Jennings	1891-1918	1945	Edd Roush	1913-1931	1962
Judy Johnson*		1975	Red Ruffing	1924-1947	1967
Walter Johnson	1907-1927	1936	Amos Rusie	1889-1901	1977
Addie Joss	1902-1910	1978	Babe Ruth	1914-1935	1936
Al Kaline	1953-1974	1980	Ray Schalk	1912-1929	1955

Career Dates indicate first and last appearances in the majors.
*Elected on the basis of his career in the Negro Leagues.

PLAYER	Career Dates	Year Selected	PLAYER	Career Dates	Year Selected
Joe Sewell	1920-1933	1977	Bobby Wallace	1894-1918	1953
Al Simmons	1924-1944	1953	Ed Walsh	1904-1917	1946
George Sisler	1915-1930	1939	Lloyd Waner	1927-1945	1967
Duke Snider	1947-1964	1980	Paul Waner	1926-1945	1952
Warren Spahn	1942-1965	1973	Monte Ward	1878-1894	1964
Tris Speaker	1907-1928	1937	Mickey Welch	1880-1892	1973
Bill Terry	1923-1936	1954	Zach Wheat	1909-1927	1959
Sam Thompson	1885-1906	1974	Ted Williams	1939-1960	1966
Joe Tinker	1902-1916	1946	Hack Wilson	1923-1934	1979
Pie Traynor	1920-1937	1948	Early Wynn	1939-1963	1971
Dazzy Vance	1915-1935	1955	Cy Young	1890-1911	1937
Rube Waddell	1897-1910	1946	Ross Youngs	1917-1926	1972
Honus Wagner	1897-1917	1936			

MANAGERS	Year Selected
Charles Comiskey	1939
Clark Griffith	1946
Bucky Harris	1974
Miller Huggins	1964
Al Lopez	1977
Connie Mack	1937
Joe McCarthy	1957
John McGraw	1937
Bill McKechnie	1962
Wilbert Robinson	1945
Casey Stengel	1974
Harry Wright	1953
George Wright	1937

SELECTED FOR MERITORIOUS SERVICE

Edward Barrow (Manager-Executive)
Morgan G. Bulkeley (Executive)
Alexander J. Cartwright (Executive)
Henry Chadwick (Writer-Statistician)
John "Jocko" Conlan (Umpire)
Thomas Connolly (Umpire)
William A. Cummings (Early Pitcher)
William G. Evans (Umpire-Executive)
Ford C. Frick (Commissioner-Executive)
Warren Giles (Executive)
William Harridge (Executive)
Cal Hubbard (Umpire)
B. Bancroft Johnson (Executive)
William Klem (Umpire)
Kenesaw M. Landis (Commissioner)
Larry S. MacPhail (Executive)
W. Branch Rickey (Manager-Executive)
Albert G. Spalding (Early Player)
George M. Weiss (Executive)
Tom Yawkey (Executive)

Career Dates indicate first and last appearances in the majors.
*Elected on the basis of his career in the Negro Leagues.

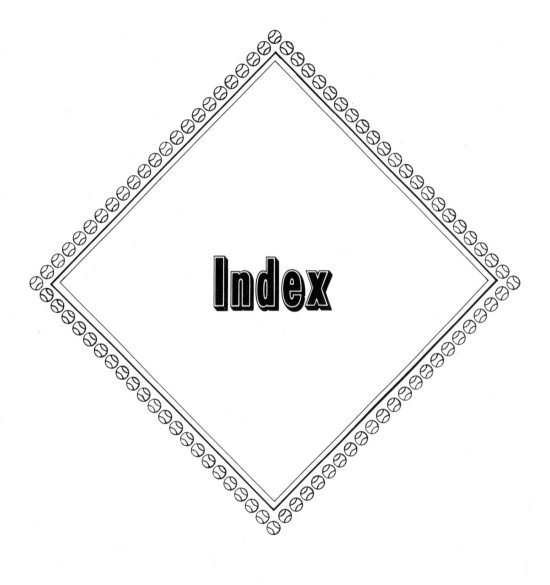

Index

Index

Numbers in italics indicate photographs.
A number followed by an "x" means that the player is listed in both the tables and the caption on that page.

INDEX

INDEX

INDEX

INDEX

INDEX

INDEX

Photo Credits